My Search for Serotonin

A BLOG

Christina Crowe

EXPERIENCES OF SUICIDAL DEPRESSION &
HOW TO DEAL WITH IT

Ottawa Canada
crowecreations.ca
info@crowecreations.ca

This book is also available in e-format.

crowecreations.ca

First Crowe Creations Edition December 2013

Designed by Crowe Creations
Text set in Arial; Headings in Times Roman

Cover design copyright © 2013 by Crowe Creations
Cover photo from iStock by Getty Images

ISBN: 978-927058-15-2

CreateSpace
ISBN-13: 978-1494827625
ISBN-10: 149482762X

Foreword

When I started writing this blog back in September of 2011, I was recovering from the effects of choices I'd made throughout my life. Life is, after all, entirely about choices. Those who fight with depression also fight with the consequences of the choices made *because* of that depression.

My depression is seasonal and I've dealt with it since before I can remember. But depression is depression. And don't let anybody tell you any different. I am lucky to be able to see myself both inside and out of it. (Although, when I'm in it, I can't see fuck-all but the darkness of The Pit.)

This book offers what I hope are healthy choices for alleviating the symptoms of depression. In no way does it offer a cure, but by the end of this blogging journey, I had finally hit on the right combination *for me*. If I help only one other person because of my own adventure in testing what works (for me) — and yes, it has been an adventure — then my effort to reach out to others like me will have been beyond worthwhile.

Hang in there. At least until you finish reading this book.

Christina
December, 2013

Dedicated to:

Lillian, Maria, and Lise.

September 4, 2011

Greetings!

I begin.

I started a blog elsewhere — from my other site — but it was very difficult to wrestle with when I wanted to actually POST something publicly. Pain in the arse for sure.

I certainly hope this site will not censor me and my wonderful sense of humour and my choice of words. (Oops, I see already that the Americans have taken over the spelling notifications.) That's okay. I won't kill myself over a battle concerning Kanucky spellings. To each his own.

Check out my website so you'll know where I'm coming from. Expect rude words:

http://crowecreations.ca/christina

Yay! Looks like it might work.

September 7, 2011

85 Days to Go

Am feeling the effects of the shortening days but am coping.

My "person" who visits every week and I had quite the conversation yesterday. In fact, I had a breakthrough.

I had been thinking (for years) that the chemicals in my brain kick in all these old negative memories that guilt the shit out of me. HOWEVER! Tada! Yesterday, I realized that I had it backwards.

(Thank you, thank you, thank you, M****, my friend and "person-who-visits" for triggering this revelation!)

It's not that my mind conjures up these things! What my mind does is dish out these horrendous guilt feelings and I — being as curious as I always am — go through my memory banks/memory drawers searching for the horrid thing that should match the feeling. But of course, I come up with nothing because I didn't do anything to warrant the feeling. At least not for the last 20 years or so. Example? Several years ago I ran over a squirrel. Remembering that can make me suicidal with guilt. But NO. I am already suicidal with "guilt" and the Squirrel Incident is what I blame it on.

Anyone else who deals with depression experience this?

I am so happy to learn that my guilt is not FOR anything, it's just there on its own, all by its stupid self. Makes it easier to deal with, I must say.

I will sign off right now and I hope to be able to wend my way back here without trouble nor grief nor bad directions.

September 11, 2011

Patience

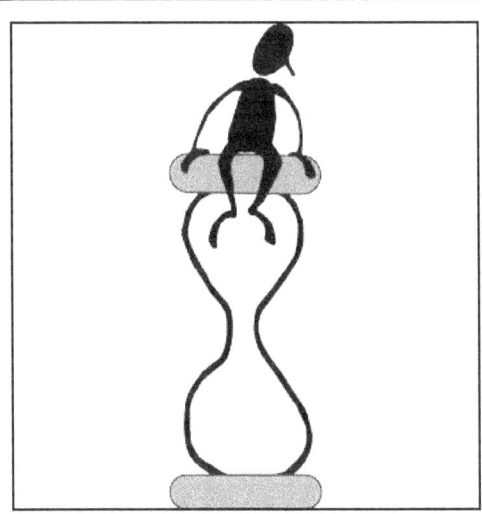

One thing I do every day is check my weight. You're not supposed to, but I do it anyway. Hey. C'mon! This satisfies my risk-taking symptom. OK? It gives me a little thrill to rebel against something even so minor. One thing I don't do every day, though, is check how many days I have left until December 1 when all this will go away again just like !THAT! Is that because I like surprises? I do, yes, but I don't check every day because it makes time slow down. For some children, the last day of school is the longest. [Actually, they aren't far off because June 21 IS the longest day — daylight-wise — but that's not what I mean, smart-ass! And I know it's sometimes June 20, smart-ass.]

Last year, on November 30, around 8 PM, I was walking toward the bathroom when it felt like somebody had poured sweet, cool water all over my brain. Right inside there. That's the best way to describe it. I could FEEL a coolness in there wash over my brain, working its way up, and I felt it all the way. All I could do was say: "Aaaaaah. Don't stop there! Don't stop there! Keep going, keep going. Aaaaaah. It's over. Done. YAY! I made it through another year!"

Lucky me, I don't lack patience. I used to, but I worked on it and learned how to develop it. See . . . It's like this: One day, many years ago, I made the mistake of PRAYING for patience. Baaaaad move, gurls and bwas, BAD move! Spirit will always give you what you ask for but not usually in the way you expect. For instance, Spirit doesn't let EVERYbody get their $1M by winning the Lottery, so when the rest of us ask for $1M, what Spirit will do is introduce you to an opportunity to make your own. And because Spirit is Spirit, getting your $1M-wish will be through your own efforts (and this is to improve your self-esteem, right?); and it will be through means which are not contrary to Universal Law; it will be eventually; and only if you work hard enough at it. How did I learn patience? How does anyone learn any skill? Practice! Yep. Another thing that Spirit has plenty of is a sense of humor. A sick one. For the next couple of years — yes YEARS! — I felt I was surely the reincarnation of Job. [That's the guy who got a whole book written about him (The Book of Job, http://en.wikipedia.org/wiki/Book_of_Job) because he made the mistake of complaining to Spirit that things in his life couldn't POSSIBLY get any worse. And this is where Spirit answered: "Ya think?"]

I learned to circumvent the anxiety of waiting, waiting, waiting by filling my life with distractions. However, I discovered early on that if these distractions were meaningless or even harmful to myself (like promiscuity or substance abuse — the other symptoms of depression) then that Guilt Thing would escalate exponentially and really fuck me up. I had to fill my life — my TIME, actually — with activities that demanded intense focus and made me feel like I'd accomplished something positive. Writing works for me. I can go into whole new worlds of my own making and do whatever I want in there. Music [during my bad time] doesn't always work for me because certain songs can bring me back to situations that made me sad*, like a break-up with Mister Right, or whatever, and any kind of grief (or anger) can trigger . . . [drum roll] . . . You got it! GUILT!

---

*Important Note: Sad is sad; depressed is depressed. Not the same thing at all.

September 12, 2011

Can't believe it. Can't believe it.

Since I had that breakthrough last week (re where cometh-from the fucking Guilt shit), I've been doing very well! It is becoming quite easy to just push it aside and tell it: "Screw off. Go elsewhere. You're not valid here, you muffer."

Am pleased with that beyond my ability to explain.

So far, so good.

If things are still the same by mid-November? Hey! Nobel Prize for moi!

September 14, 2011

Look What I Found!

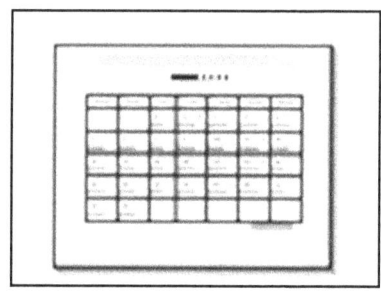

☺

http://www.sunrisesunset.com/ Pick your city and you make a calendar (well, it's automatic) showing sunrise and sunset and a bunch of stuff about the moon and astronomical data, etc. Cool.

September 16, 2011

76 Days to Go

Time flies, eh? Seventy-six days. Just over two months. Since June 21 (when the days start to get shorter), we've gotten through July . . . August . . . part of September already . . . Getting there.

I'm still doing well with my New Attitude, my New Viewpoint from inside The Head. It's working. Can't believe it!

I remember now that my brother spoke to me one time about this nebulous Guilt that floated around him too, like the cloud that follows Pig-Pen (Peanuts) around:

http://en.wikipedia.org/wiki/Pig-Pen

He drank to assuage the Guilt and his Superego (provided by Mommy Dearest's voice) provided the guilt for drinking in the first place. "Bad boy. Just like your evil father who spent money on beer once a week and I had to dig lipstick out of the tube so I

could continue to look amazingly beautiful in my extremely expensive clothes." The pattern is: Anger -> Guilt -> Depression -> Anger -> Guilt -> Depression ad infinitum or until you can grab one of those stages and wrestle the bastid into submission. And I am not talking about suppressing one of these stages. That's the worst thing you can do because it just hides in there and feeds on you and grows and grows and you aren't even aware it's doing that. Then, when you least expect it, it comes roaring out of the pit to strangle you, or slash your wrists, or feed you a bunch of pills. I used to call mine The Mean Little Kid. What a proper bitch she was. She hated me. She did everything in her power to do damage to me. I had nightmares of her with teeth like Alien (the movie). I'd be on a bus, perhaps, and I wouldn't notice that she was behind me. Then before I could react, she would grab me and dig those 6-inch-long teeth into the back of my neck. Scary shit, my anger. Scaaaary!

September 19, 2011

Do What Makes You Feel Good about Yourself

I have a friend whose life for the last several years was a little bit blank for her because she had somebody telling her what to think and what to do.

Duh.

And I am not meaning that my friend is "duh", far from it. Her now [thank the gods] ex-companione was duh. We Depressives tend to get mixed up with assholes ALL the time. We know flipping better but it satisfies that Substance Abuse/Risk Taking/Promiscuity thing that Depressives have to deal with. I don't know if she suffers from — or even enjoys [laugh laugh] — Depression, but I'm going to use her as an example of What Not To Do.

It actually feels really good to wallow and believe that we are to blame for everything from measles to the Holocaust. Baaah! We are not. No matter what your Lover (and I use that term in the loosest of fashions) tells you, you are NOT to blame for the fucking Holocaust. Christ-a-mighty! You probably weren't even alive then. And even if you were, you can't do dick-all about it now. You should have done something then, when you were what? 10 years old? Minus 10 years old? Minus 20 years old? Fuck!

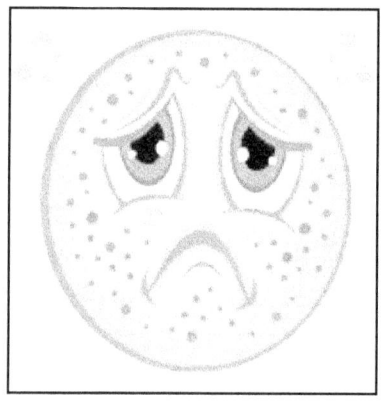

However . . . Little kids can grow up to change the world. My mentor was a Hippy. Those guys accomplished amazing things because they believed in Right and Not Right and did something about it — that was that whole Age of Aquarius shit where you questioned stuff and protested the hell out of everything. You asked yourself stuff like why is it OK for the government to lie to us but we aren't allowed to lie to the government, and you bitched about it OUT LOUD. Amazingly, shit changed.

You are capable of that kind of power, too. All you need to do is believe in yourself. Yeah. Yeah. Yeah.

btw, It is NOT a sin to do something that empowers you. It is NOT a sin to do what makes you feel good. (Well, aside from doing weird things to dead bodies, that is . . . or inflicting pain on another Earthling. — And "Earthling" includes bugs, too. nyah!)

Note: Mosquitoes don't count.

September 27, 2011

My other other "job" . . .

All right. So I have "other" stuff I do.

I dog-/house-sit when I am/am not writing.

This makes me have good self-esteem because I have my own business. Wow. That empowers the shit out of you if you have your own business. If you only — like "only" — babysit, then that's a business. You can do your thing with Revenue Canada if you have Your Own Business*. It is really easy to register your own business, too. (Go here:

http://www.registerbusinessinontario.com/Business-registration.html?gclid=CLu-1vrnvqsCFQUCQAod5UVluw)

Okay, so this is what I wrote to a bunch of my friends when I was away dog-sitting this past week. Doing business. Dealing. Improving my lot. Having a fucking HOOT!

Hi all y'all

Am still in boonies for another day or so with my 13 precious little charges. Will be extremely glad to get home because it feels like a workout at the gym just to feed them, or put them to bed, or get up and down every time one of them wants out to pee. (Um . . . 13 x 200 times/hour = . . .) That's lots of lifting, and bending of rarely used body parts, and stairs. (Their sleeping area is in the basement.) And the stairs are done while actually carrying one really old guy (Jerry) who, when I'm carrying him, can't wag his tail so he wags his leg instead. Try navigating steep basement stairs while laughing.

Yesterday, I looked over to see old Jennie scratching her ear. The breed is notable for the hairiness of their ears. This is Jazz as an idea for those of you who are unfamiliar with the breed. Please note blurred tail. Her ears are fairly short because one of the young ones has decided he likes chewing ear hair. I am to watch for that and spray gross stuff on ears if I catch him at it. Luckily though, since I've been here, he's more interested in the squirrels outside so spends the whole day slobbering all over his ruff and barking. In humans, this leads to psychosis. I'm not sure what it does to puppies. I'm not sure at this point if I'm worried, either.

So I keep looking at Jennie because something isn't quite right. Every time she scratches her ear, her head bobs. Oh. I see now. She has her toenail caught in her ear hair. (I know some guys like that. lol) Now where did my client tell me she keeps the scissors?

I don't know how my client does it but she can feed all 13 of them simultaneously, 9 in the same room. Hell! I am only just learning to tell them apart! And that's with mug shots provided by my client. On Thursday, I fed Massy (the hog) twice. (The little liar!) So now what I do is stick the two who ARE fed in a crate in their crates, feed them, then find another dog, match with photo and with the food they are supposed to get — two elderly ones are on a special medical diet so can't eat anybody else's and vice versa — and put two more in. And out. "This is not the way Mommy does it, Auntie Chistina." Jennie and Stella get fed outside the kitchen gate (standard, not just when I'm here). So I figured I'd feed Massy and Hatty out there when the regular girls were finished. Brilliant, because Massy and Hatty try to eat everybody else's food after they've vacuumed down their own, anyway. Bonus.

Oh, and I also have to put snoods on certain ones so they don't get their ears gobbed up by their food because they are dog show regulars.

So I put Massy and Hatty out there, they ate in 2 seconds flat, and I'm in the kitchen, the dog room off the kitchen, opening and closing the door to let this one and that one in or out, and organizing this and that, and carrying dogs and juggling dishes in . . . my third hand? And I look over to see Massy and Hatty watching me through the gate like visitors at a zoo. I had to put the dog I was holding back onto the floor I got to laughing so hard.

Yes. I'll be glad to get home but I'll be just as glad to come back again next time.

(And what's this business about you feeling insecure? If you have your own business, even if it is just plucking feathers from a discarded pillow, and if you only make 2 pennies per 10,000 feathers, it's still YOUR BUSINESS, isn't it?

September 30, 2011

Tick Tock

Yup. The days are getting shorter quicker. If you don't already have a special light, check this site out:

http://www.northernlighttechnologies.ca/home#!__home

I've had a SADelite for nearly 10 years now. It cost me ~$245.00 back then and I got a new one a couple of years ago for the same price (but now then there's the HST) — however, you can, apparently, get some kind of insurance benefit or something. You'd have to check that out on your own. These Northern Light Technologies people deliver at warp speed. (Montreal based.) They also deliver replacement lights at warp speed, too. The lights last a very long time and only use the same as a regular light bulb would.

This light has saved my life for years.

They recommend that you sit in front of it for 1/2 hour or so early in the morning to start off your day, as this will tell your amygdalae (the Lizard Brain http://en.wikipedia.org/wiki/ Amygdala) that the day is longer than they thought it was. Peeps with blue eyes have to be more careful with it. It's hella bright! This 1/2-hour thing would be for peeps who have to go off to work. There are smaller ones you can take to work with you and there's even one that looks like a baseball cap with lights under the cap.

I work from home so I try to make myself wake up around 6 AM — more difficult to do when it's dark at that time — to turn my light on. It fills the whole living room with fake sunlight and wakes me up and makes me smile.

Warning: Do NOT get overly enthusiastic about this sweet darling of a light and leave it on into the evening because it is SO effective, it'll keep you awake all night! I know whereof I speak. lol

(63 days to go. Woohoo!)

October 3, 2011

This is cool . . .

It's the Real Age Test. Try it out. I do it once a year.

http://www.care2.com/greenliving/7-ways-to-train-your-brain-to-sleep-better-naturally.html

October 12, 2011

Time flies . . .

. . . when your day is jammed with doing things that keep you so busy you wonder just how much of a masochist you are. But here I am on Day 50 already! Hard to believe.

I am still forcing myself to get up at 6 AM to turn on My Light and bask in it. Working great. But I am still forcing away those damn Guilties that I wake up with every morning, though.

Last week, I received a lovely notebook from a friend and I've dedicated it as a new Dream Diary. Haven't been able to write any more in it but the date and "Nothing remembered again this morning. Poo." So don't know what dreams are going on in there that do this guilt thing to me. I will try an experiment tonight — if I remember. [Note to Christina: REMEMBER!] The experiment will be to dream nice things. I always conjure up nice things at bedtime and push away any negatives. I used to try to spend a million dollars. I'm up to trying to spend a billion now. Inflation! And that helps me to sleep instead of tossing and turning for hours. When I wake up in the middle of the night, I go back to building fancy highrises in my head, ones with roof gardens and lots and lots of windows to let the light in.

A counsellor told me once that I should write down the thoughts of the day on a piece of paper before bedtime. I think that's a way of setting them aside. The concept is that you wrap your prayer request ("When You Wish upon a Star") in a little package and put it on the altar where it will be dealt with. This is quite healthy, actually. You get it out of yourself. And the idea is to forget about it once it's on the altar. It's somebody else's concern now. It's quite amazing that the Somebody else usually takes care of it.

If you are worried about something ask yourself: "What will it matter 50 years from now?"

October 19, 2011

Bummer!

We lost another young one in Ottawa over the weekend to suicide. He was a month short of his 16th birthday. He had a challenge to deal with and on top of the challenge itself, he was bullied for it. Decided it was better to jump ship. Unfortunate. In that state, you sometimes think: "I'll make them feel guilty for being mean to me." Trouble is, they are not the ones who will end up feeling guilty. They're assholes who'll grow up to be wife-beaters, or big-moneyed corporation heads, or prison inmates. The ones who'll feel guilty will be the ones who love you. Maybe even people you didn't know about.

Many times we don't want to actually kill ourselves, we just want whatever it is to stop. I've been there. Where there seems like no other option. You get tired fighting it. You just plain old give up. Say "Fuck it, I'm outta here."

Depression itself tires you out, weakens you. Came across this link a day or so ago:

http://www.sharecare.com/health/sleep-disorders/article/5-foods-that-help-you-sleep-better

Looks like it has some good ideas for bed-time munchies that will help you sleep better, at least. A start. Right? I'm tossing and turning now even though I follow my own advice by priming the pump of interesting ideas to dream of while sleeping. When I wake up in the middle of the night (very often, now that November is approaching), I try to plan out one of my stories.

Whether you write or not, it might be a good thing to cultivate, but do it on paper that can easily be ripped up into teeny pieces and tossed. I was writing in a diary/journal in high school — had already filled three of them — but my mother got hold of them. She was more interested in what I had to say about HER than in any of my problems, but she still made my life pure hell by constantly harping on what she'd read. When you have a narcissist for a mommy and she projects herself onto you and she doesn't like herself, she doesn't like you either. I never, ever felt that Mom loved me. Or even liked me or what I did. But in retrospect, why would I care that a woman incapable of love didn't love me? Yeah, but it was my MOTHER! Looking back on my life, I see that I went through a series of men who were incapable of love. "As the twig is bent . . ."*

You can go through your whole life blaming Mommy Dearest (or whomever) for the way your life sucks. Or you can shape your life into the way you want it in spite of how your twig was bent when you were growing up.

Next time, I'll tell you about the concept of The Guf (also, Guff, Guph) where little souls wait to be born.

---

*Just as the Twig is bent, the Tree's inclined. (1732 Pope *Epistles to Several Persons I.* 102).

October 22, 2011

The Chamber of Guf

... or Guff, or Guph, the spelling doesn't matter, it's the concept"

http://en.wikipedia.org/wiki/Guf

The Concept. Many people get so caught up in the details of things they miss the underlying concept of it all. I'm not talking about sensible stuff like driving on the proper side of the road, but things like "I pray to God not to Allah." Well . . . Duh. In Arabic, the word for God IS Allah. [the god, meaning the one and only as in monotheistic like Judaism and Christianity and that's why these three religious groups are so closely knit. They're cousins. And each of these groups has its own set of nut cases. Don't try to deny it!] That's like a French person saying: "I pray to Dieu not to God" and having somebody get all knotted up about that. Can you picture some gossip whispering: "He's Spanish. He prays to Dios so he's going straight to Hell when he dies."?

The Chamber of Guf:

The concept is that our consciousness, our souls, our spirits, our divine spark, our psis come from somewhere. The concept of The Guf is the best explanation I've found so far. I have my own picture of it — I'm a writer, I see things and I try to see them from my own perspective uncoloured by programming or societal pressures. (Not easy but I try.) This makes me appear to be a bit off the wall but people respect me for it. (Not easy but they try.) I don't judge them, either. (Usually easy, but sometimes trying.)

What I see is a vast hallway of little souls jostling around happily, content, and full of the purest love imaginable. They are all tiny pieces of the Whole.

I see some guy with a clipboard up front. (You can put glasses on him if you want. Next shift, it might be a gal with big boobs and an annoying nasal twang to her voice. Doesn't matter. Concept, okay?) So this guy is reading specifications off his clipboard and while he goes down the list the crowd grows quiet. Looks like the next available babybody will be a tough assignment.

Mister Clipboard looks up over his glasses to survey the group. Nobody will make eye contact with him. It seems everyone has stopped breathing.

"Well?" His eyebrows wriggle. "Any takers? I know it'll be a difficult gig, but we need a volunteer."

Way in the back a little hand shoots up. "I'll do it!" And an ooh of approval murmurs through the crowd.

As the volunteer comes to the front of the line, there is much back-slapping and encouraging words. "Good for you." "You're a brave one." "And volunteering to be a female on top of everything else? That takes guts in that neighborhood!" "If I run into you down there, I'll try to help you." "Yeah. I'll help, too. I'll try to grab the next available babybody for that neighborhood. We can maybe get married, eh?" The volunteer giggles. Blushes. Steps forward. Takes a deep breath and off it goes into the World of Earth.

(40 days to go)

October 26, 2011

Migrate or Hibernate

Feel familiar at all?

I heard that we depressives get depressed even more if we can't migrate or hibernate when we see the squirrels getting down to business and the crows singing that special song of theirs and when the tree leaves start to lose that beautiful green lustre and start to yellow at the edges. A vee of geese honks southward and we reach for the closest bottle, pill, noose, gun ... when we might better be reaching for the closest travel agent's phone number or going shopping for freezables.

If you want chickens to keep laying, you maintain the length of day artificially. Birds evolved to fly to sunnier climes and we've massaged the poor chicken into sticking around. We must therefore, offer them some hope.

Inadequate daylength: Hens need about 14 hours of daylength to maintain egg production. The intensity of light should be sufficient to allow a person to read newsprint at bird level. The decreasing daylength during the Fall and shorter daylengths in the Winter would be expected to cause a severe decline, or even cessation, in egg production unless supplemental light is provided. When production ceases, the birds may also undergo a feather molt. Hens exposed to only natural light would be expected to resume egg production in the Spring. (University of Florida IFAS Extension, Solutions for Your Life, EDIS, Publication # PS-35. Factors Affecting Egg Production in Backyard Chicken Flocks, J.P. Jacob, H.R. Wilson, R.D. Miles, G.D. Butcher, and F.B. Mather)

I'm not much of a traveler. We moved so much when I was a kid that I'm kinda burnt out as far as wanting "to explore strange new worlds, to seek out new life forms and new civilizations, to boldly go where no one has gone before" goes, so I tend to hibernate. Although I didn't know that's what I was leaning toward until I began examining my depression more closely in recent years. What do I do now? I shop for freezables. I buy family-sized packages of lasagna, Vietnamese soup, cabbage rolls, hmm that looks good, too ... Into the basket it goes. Then, squirrel-like, once I get everything back home, I open all the packages, divide them into meal-sized portions and tuck them away in my freezer. I've been doing this for the last several years and it has actually lessened that stress-ish feeling I get around this time of year. The guilt I feel — and depressive guilt uses every opportunity it can to express itself [see, Friday, 16 Sept. 2011 post] — for "spending all that money" doesn't last long when I divide the number of packages by what I've spent and end up with a tidy little sum between $2-3 per meal, often less. Chocolate doesn't count! That's another post entirely.

Here are a few links:

http://www.foodsfordepression.net/
http://www.naturalnews.com/020611.html
http://www.foodforthebrain.org/content.asp?id_Content=1635
http://www.webmd.com/depression/guide/diet-recovery

I stock up on cans of tuna and salmon. No need to make a sandwich out of them (they say carbs add to belly bulge! as does stress), I put a can's worth into a bowl with a bit of pepper (pinch or two of dill on the salmon), and there I have a healthy, mood-boosting graze. (A friend calls me a grazer because I don't eat regular meals. I'll eat some cheese, an hour later maybe a banana and/or grapes, then a bagel, then some fruit, chew on some carrot sticks, etc. But I don't care how much she teases me, it's supposed to be healthier to ingest our dietary needs spread throughout the day. Work hours and other traditions tend to force us into eating regularly, something I resent because we depressives tend to be rebellious. I don't know about you, but I need to get my serotonin boost wherever I can. If defying tradition by eating the way I want to gives me a jolt, so be it. (Remember, the signs of depression are: substance abuse, promiscuity, and risk taking. These vary in degree among individuals, of course. Rebellion serves my risk-taking need quite nicely. Beats getting involved with disturbed men who own guns like I used to. Right?)

I eat when I'm hungry . . .

Now, see? What my mind wants to do is continue on with that old song: "I eat when I'm hungry, I drink when I'm dry, and if moonshine don't kill me, I'll live till I die." This annoying aspect of my depression tends to kick in around October 26. Ah. Right on time, aren't we? Fine! Only 36 more days to deal with it.

November 1, 2011

The Full-blown Stupids

I'm right into the thick of it. Ah, well, fewer than one-third of the days left than when I started counting this go around.

Getting a handle on The Guilt Thing is really helping out this year, but I am NOT going to let my guard down for one teeny second.

When I was living with the most-recent ex, The Bad Time started earlier and earlier every year (even backing up to June/July toward the end). It's wonderful now that it's settled down once again to starting around October 26. I kid you not. It starts and ends almost on cue (as long as I'm not dealing with heavy stress factors). I wonder if it's related to Sun in Scorpio? I am not "adversely aspected" Astrology-wise when the Sun is in Scorpio so maybe it's something my Lizard Brain remembers from when it used to be a silly goose? (Insert smiley face here, please.)

What I'm Noticing:

- memory slips (examples: forgetting the name of a movie; forgetting where I left that, uh . . . what was it I was looking for? and then forgetting I was looking for something in the first place; forgetting routine tasks or whether I already did them or not)
- easily frustrated with usually forgivable things
- I'm waking up every hour on the hour while trying to sleep
- lack of enthusiasm about stuff I normally love doing
- general aches and pains (I am getting older, but it seems worse during The Bad Time)
- something might trigger a tune in my head and then I can't get it to stop fucking PLAYING! (^%&%$!*#$)
- sex drive in the negative numbers

Suggestions for Dealing:

- write notes; plant stickies all over the place if something's all that important. Try to remember if it was important to you when you weren't in Your Bad Time and if not, try to forget about it. Remind yourself there will be an end to it in x number of days. (I realize that not all depressions are blessedly seasonal, so for some, it looks like it will never end. Work out something that gives you hope. Examples: next doctor's visit; Fridays; paydays; TV shows you like; etc.)

- breathe. Distract yourself with something you like doing. This isn't easy if you're at work and what's frustrating you sits at the one-over desk. If you have an office job, you might consider discussing with your boss the possibility of working from home during Your Bad Time. If that's not possible, you need to get involved in something that helps vent your frustrations. Exercise is supposed to be good for that as it gets the ol' serotonin running like sap in a spring maple. What I did one year (back in the days) was write a book. When I'd come home from work, I'd continue with the story and develop another victim in the book and kill him/her off. The book never made it to print but I got some fantastic benefits from it: I realized I could finish something as demanding as a book; I got thoughts of killing (myself-instead-of-them) out of my head and onto paper which contributed toward a finished book and might have saved an actual life (mine) by taking a made-up one; I am developing at least three screenplays (movies) from that book! How great is that? Note: Do NOT use real people in your stories. Make up characters by exaggerating your frustrating colleague's faults to the nth degree. Change the sex of that person, the occupation, the town, the race, the weight, hair and eye color, etc. The idea is not to kill that particular person in your writing, it's to get the hostility OUT OF YOU. It's actually a lot of fun to make up a character with an exaggerated trait, then have the Fates deal with them. Make one a bug — a very bossy bug, or a gossipy bug, or a lying bug that has a fight with another bug and runs out of the bug restaurant (or wherever) and gets smucked on a windshield. What you are doing is personifying the annoying trait — not the person — and killing off the annoying trait.

- losing sleep is bad for us depressives and short of taking drugs, it looks like we have to deal with it until Our Bad Time is over. We need only remind ourselves when we wake up, that there will be an end to it, that once this particular night is over, that means we have gotten one day closer to the end. I mentioned in another post about thinking of pleasant things like spending a billion dollars. Whatever you do, don't rehash the Bad Thing or make plans for dealing with Annoying People during the night. That'll give you nightmares for sure. Don't allow yourself to think of ANYthing negative. Imagine going to a tropical island (you can afford it, you have a billion dollars to spend, right?) or climb Everest or whatever you'd enjoy doing, then drift off to sleep again (for another hour or so).

- enthusiasm will return when The Bad Time is over. Right now it doesn't feel like it whatsoever, so I am only talking from experience, not from what I right-at-the-moment think I know for sure. Suggest you try to hold onto that good thought, too

- aches and pains? Get an exercise program going and blame them on that. You don't need to join a gym or anything. Here's my list, and don't laugh at my terminology. Or, go ahead and laugh. Laughing's good for us. I do these at the kitchen counter (there's a corner where my knees fit when I bend) while the coffee's running through. Once or twice a day if or whenever: 10 knee bends (mine are not very deep yet); 10 heel lifts; 10 push aways (vertical push-ups. I do these by holding onto the sink. Started with my feet about 30 cm back and have now increased that to ~45 cm); 10 door hangs (I'm tall so I can hold onto the lip-thing over a door and lean forward, holding for a bit, then onto #2, etc.); 10 kitty lifts (I hold my cat under his front legs and his belly and lift him up over my head. No cat? Use two cans of tomatoes or beans or something lying around). These "exercises" mostly involve stretching. Think up your own or buy a yoga book and do some of those. Just remember, no pressure on yourself to do these. Remember The Guilt Thing always. Don't get involved in ANYthing that might contribute to The Guilt Thing.

- tunes in my head? Once again, distraction usually works. Comfort yourself with the knowledge that some people hear voices all the time unless they're on their meds. Things could always be worse

- this too shall pass. Although . . . one of the symptoms of clinical depression is promiscuity so if you have the opposite situation — an increase in your sex drive — stock up on condoms and forget about taking risks in that area of your life! You're not the only one involved in THIS risk. Think of your partners. Please.

Hang in there.

November 2, 2011

Jeepers

Everything, just everything, is so damned difficult. Standing up hurts. Even picking up the TV remote is exhausting, mostly because I have trouble deciding what I want to switch to once I do, nothing interests me. Breathing is work. I am forced to use my puffer which I never use. I get them, then have to throw them out unused because they're past the best-by date. I smoked for years, you see. Did in my lungs (emphysema and asthma). (Substance abuse.) Hung with heavy smokers/boozers. (Risk taking.)

I'm happy to see TV commercials these days which describe the symptoms of depression. This means depression is coming out of its black hole.

No closet this! Closets have doors. Even in horror movies, closets have doors — although, for some reason, they often get locked but only when somebody's in one. As an aside, tell me, please. What house have you ever been in with locks on any door but the bathroom and maybe Mommy and Daddy's room? Ditto for those movie-set closet doors with the slats in them for children to watch brutal murders through. Oops. Have I ruined every horror movie you ever saw? My apologies, but because I write in this genre, I am extra diligent in watching for glitches. In horror stories, and especially in sci-fi, the Suspension of Disbelief is paramount.

But back to the commercials. During my Normal Time while watching these commercials and hearing that "depression hurts", I always said to myself: "Not me. It doesn't do anything physical to me. How lucky I am." But now that I have that annoying Guilt Thing under a smidgen of control, I am better able to see what else goes on with my body, and I am very, very surprised to learn that depression DOES affect one's entire system. Good to know. Nothing all that serious then, right? All in our heads? It's as serious as a guillotine.

Some scientific group or other did a study on the brains of people who were both depressive and suicidal. (Apparently one can be severely depressed but non-suicidal. That would not be me. I am suicidal. And, uh, this testing is done in laboratories, eh? Not on living subjects?) In the brains of those with both symptoms they found extra receptors. From what I understand, extra receptors means an extra need for serotonin and those other feel-good chemicals. Our bodies produce these normally. For us depressive-suicidal types, the normal amount is not enough because our brains want more. So we seek serotonin boosts: substance abuse, promiscuity, and risk taking. Not one of these is a good idea if you look closely at what can happen if Something Goes Wrong. Having an inkling of why we might do these things will make us feel less guilty about having done them, though. Hooray, hooray, it's not my fault. Hooray, hooray. Now what we need do is concentrate on finding substitutes for these possibly dangerous activities — substitutes which are just as much fun. Not an easy task. And it's entirely individual. Me? I write. Some people sing. Some dance. Some exercise. Some bird-watch. Do your own thing. Only you know what will work for you.

November 3, 2011

Space bends?

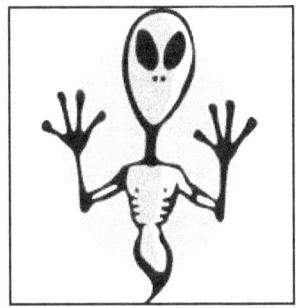

We all thought that Space was a vacuum, didn't we? Turns out it ain't. I've been watching programs lately which discuss Physics — particularly Quantum Mechanics. (Don't tell anybody, but I love this shit.) Because I'm a writer, my right brain (concept side) gets a regular daily workout, so I can actually follow this stuff even though it's a total mind-fuck.

In school, I had a problem with Arithmetic from the get-go because I moved mid-first-year into a district where they were already adding and subtracting numbers, so I was lost. Plus, unfortunately, the way my mind worked was that I could quickly glance at a problem (1 + 3, for example) and come up with the Close-Enough-For-Me Answer partly because Mrs. Teacher had put that same particular problem on the board just a couple of days ago. I had always relied on memory and concept, but Arithmetic required left-brain work. My subconscious told me not to get involved with all those schtewpud time-wasting numbers when a guess was close enough.

As it turned out, the stress of failing at something did a real number on my Arithmetic self-esteem so anything Math-ish, I ran from, screaming. Later on in life, when I became aware of Quantum Mechanics a.k.a. Quantum Physics, I kicked my arse HARD for eschewing Arithmetic when I had my chance to embrace it. Life is all about choices, isn't it?

Why am I talking about Quantum Mechanics? Because everything affects everything else. All that empty Space out there isn't empty after all but full of things that bounce around and appear and disappear and annihilate each other constantly. It's what they call Dark Energy/Dark Matter and they haven't a clue what it is. How fascinating is that? Stuff appears out of nowhere! Seventy percent of our Universe is made of this non-stuff! They know it exists because it affects things they CAN see and measure, but they can't PROVE it's actually there. For some reason, this makes my soul giggle.

What I'm wanting to say in this post is that WE affect everything around us, too. WE are 70% Dark Matter. On the program "How Long Is a Piece of String?" one of the physicists stated that if you took all the Space out of all the molecules of every human on earth, what's left would be the size of a sugar cube. That's a lot of nothing that was walking around, eating, singing, loving. Being.

Lately, things have been screwing up. One of my computer's programs ceased working properly; then another one; when I did the laundry last week, one load ended up a sopping mess because the spin cycle hadn't worked; one of my not-for-profit clients has had a financial downturn so won't be using my services for a while; a little thing here, a little thing there . . .

So what I got to thinking was that the Fates were beating up on me. Woe is me. As if I don't have enough problems at this time of year. Boo hoo. Like the weak one in the pack, the others are going to kill me and toss my body to the scavengers.

But then I remembered how lucky I am usually. How things always seem to go my way if I just "ask". I'm not talking about official, religious praying here, or making wishes, I'm talking about needing something and sending out the vibe that I'm going to get it. The converse is also true: If I expect the worst to happen, it will. We affect everything around us whether we are aware of it or not. So here's another thing we must try to do during The Bad Time. Think positive. Expect the best. Maybe "the best" won't happen, but this attitude will help keep the negative things at bay until we're feeling better and attracting the positive things once again.

November 7, 2011

ohhhh shit

Right now what I'm wanting to do is go to the building beside mine. It has 18 floors. And jump off the roof. And I can get there easily. Really easily and that scares the shit out of me because I don't really want to do it but there's something else inside me that is making me want to do it REALLY BADLY.

Gawd I hate this time of year!

November 10, 2011

I'm okay.

Wow. That sucked!

I fought it off and was okay by the next morning.

I used to have that feeling 24/7 so getting it once in a while is great. HOWEVER, it's like when you're not used to something — let's say running 20 kms? — and then it happens, it wipes you right out. Scared hell outta me, anyway, with its power.

There's good news though. That bad night (Monday), because I'd been having such trouble sleeping in my own bed, I switched to the couch, just for the night. Tossed and turned (but hey, what was different about that, eh?), however, when I woke up, I felt rested. And that horrible urge was gone. Still felt like crap, though. Stiff and sore and tired. Unbelievably TIRED.

Then on Tuesday night, when I lay down, it felt like my lungs were full of fluid. I couldn't breathe. Thought I was going to die. Wondered how I could talk on 911 if I happened to begin suffocating totally. Now what the hell was happening to me? I got up and used my puffer. It seemed to help but when I lay flat again, I still couldn't breathe. I was very tired (like I said) and was practically falling asleep, needed the sleep. I grabbed a bunch of sofa cushions and propped myself up to sleep that way. Gradually throughout the night I removed cushion after cushion until I was down to two levels by the morning.

The crazy thing is, that when I woke up the next morning (Wednesday), I was in such a good mood. It seemed like The Bad Time was gone. Today — this will sound really, really asinine — I can feel it in my eyebrows. Yes, my eyebrows. They are relaxed today. Last night (or was it the night before?) I thought I felt that "lifting" in my head but couldn't believe it could be happening so soon. Usually it's not until December 1. But we've had such a beautiful November. Sunny, warm, etc. Maybe it took The Bad Time away? I'm not letting down my guard though. Not yet. Even though it goes away December 1, I'm only talking about the really BAD stuff that's hard to control (like wanting to jump). It stays there until the days start to get longer around December 21 and improves gradually until the sun shines brightly early and into the evenings.

btw, when I wanted to jump, it wasn't to die — not at all — it was to feel the splat. Like I wanted to "hit" myself really hard, make it hurt. I'll think on this and letchaz know.

November 12, 2011

Some good ideas ...

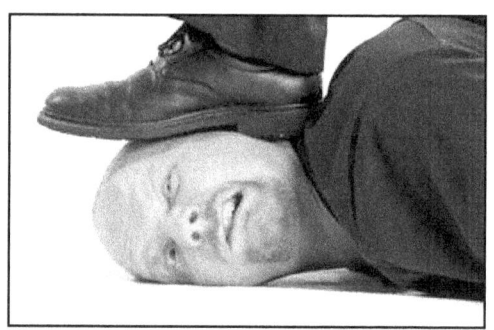

... on handling stress (a.k.a. feeling crappy about life):

http://www.realage.com/health-tips/3-steps-to-coping-with-stress?eid=1010648469&memberid=50181327

November 20, 2011

Still here

I'm back home from another dog-sitting gig. Got home earlier than expected so BONUS.

Feeling good. Am usually fighting good this time of year, but am feeling good instead. This is wonderful. Can't believe it, actually. Must be because of all the sunny, warm days we had in November this year in this area that The Bad Time lifted early. I don't care WHY, I'm just happy THAT. Still not letting my guard down, though — have 11 days to go until December 1. And especially not turning off my light! And I still have the stupids but am not as "depressed" about that as usual. ha ha (Hey, look! I made a funny.)

It helps with the dog-sitting because I know how important I am to them. The dogs, I mean. Dogs always like you no matter what so they're easy to be around for us depressives.

This dog-sitting gig was for a different client. These are not that huge pack of little happy tail-waggers, these are five large hunting-type dogs (not hounds) with practically unexpendable energy: go go go go go. Two of them just turned 13 and for large breeds, this is equivalent to about 110 in human years.

Seems my vacation is over now and it will be back to work tomorrow. And I have shit-loads to do. That could be depressing but I'm forcing myself to look at it as being needed.

Hang in there.

November 28, 2011

3 Days to Go!

Here I am having [so far so good] made it through another Bad Time. But one always must maintain vigilance during these days.

If you recall, I was feeling really good there for a while. But I got a little cocky. Since last week, the days have been their usual-November overcast, but because I was feeling so well, I did some this-n-that away from the influence of my precious light. I guess you could say about me: "She's okay unless she goes off her light." ha ha Went through some guilt-tripping shit yesterday. Had attended a local fundraiser dinner and dance on Saturday night with A Special Friend as escort so was on a relative high until I opened an email on Sunday morning that got me all Guilt-Ridden. Kaboom! Back into the depths we go.

I belong to several organizations and associations. For one of these, our group used to hold seasonal parties at a member's home way out in the boonies where "nobody can hear you scream" if you get my drift. We are always recruiting members, we have an e-mag that goes out to members only, but a newsletter that goes out on a public mailing list. The member is a wonderful, loving, accepting, therefore somewhat naive person who, at first, saw no harm in publicly advertising where she lives.

I jumped in with: "You really want to tell every potential cyberspacer that you have expensive shit in your house and you live alone way out there?"

She responded with: "Oh. Heh. Right."

Thanks to the generous offer of a member, last year we changed venues to a city location to make the party more accessible (in case of Canadian weather on the party day) and were particularly careful not to publicly advertise where this member's apartment building (party room) was, and therefore, where she lives. We provided her email address for folks to RSVP and (once vetted) to acquire directions to this new hostess's building. The email I opened yesterday morning was to announce that this year, directions to the party were going to be sent out to everyone on the mailing list to encourage All And Sundry to show up. Umm. Tap, tap on shoulder. "Guys? More than the members will get this, eh?"

"Oh," responded one person. "Yeah. Heh. Right."

"Well, it's too late now!" responded the person who sends these things out who happens to be a really good friend of mine. Not angrily as it might appear, but with total shock that she might have inadvertently sentenced some sweet, elderly woman to horrors beyond imagination just by following what seems on the face of it to be an extremely logical and innocent suggestion by the original no-one-can-hear-you-scream hostess.

So here I am, racked with guilt about making my friend feel guilty about sending out this message to the public.

So why am I so paranoid? I'm not paranoid. It's called hypervigilance and it's a symptom of PTSD (Post Traumatic Stress Disorder). I was stalked by an abusive ex-boyfriend (whose brother-in-law had a shed-full of big whonking guns (AK-47s?) one of which my ex-boyfriend pointed at me and pulled the trigger to 'splain what would happen to me if I ever opened my mouth about what I had just accidentally seen. That was in Another Life. See my previous comments about depressives and Risk Taking . . . If you haven't guessed yet, that's my biggee: risk taking. I should be dead. I really should be dead. The guy was also a druggie. He's not the only scary person I've been involved with. He was the only terrorist, though. (And before you RCMP guys who might be reading this get all excited, this was many, many years ago and you guys already know everything about him.)

It's plain old common sense, too. They teach this stuff to diplomats and high-ranking officials to avoid their getting . . . like . . . assassinated? Their kids kidnapped? You know, the kind of drama that only happens in the movies? Never in real life. And it doesn't happen in real life because they are VIGILANT about not have set routines, giving out personal information like where you can be found if any flipping sociopath wants to take a few minutes out of his day to track you down and have some his-kind-of-fun with your dead body. Or just steal all your stuff.

Following my stalking episode (one-and-a-half years of it), I learned a lot more when I had to get a certain Security Clearance for where I worked. So high that some dude from the RCMP came to give us A Little Talk. He said "You must give out NO information whatsoever. What they do is get a tidbit of information from him, a little from her, a little from you. One of his buddies will get a snippet from him, and him, and her. Then they have a meeting, compare all these seemingly small, insignificant bits of information, and they'll have the whole picture."

"Oh. Heh. Right."

Thanks for listening. I feel better.

December 1, 2011

Made it!

Nothing seems any different really but I didn't wake up feeling guilty-about-nothing this morning. Major plus, that. Yay!

I have a ton of stuff to do today so can't write long. Have to go downtown (buses REALLY suck this time of year as everybody is Christmas shopping) so want to get it over with. They have this special deal for Ottawa buses. Seniors get to ride free on Wednesdays and on Monday and Friday afternoons. Picture this at front of bus while driver pulls away then slams on the brakes, then pulls away again: two sets of strollers and three walkers and you're trying to squish through this ALSO jammed-full bus of regulars to grab an upright pole rather than swing on a strap near the front like a monkey all without falling against some pervert who probably, full of hope, rides the buses. ha

Later.

December 2, 2011

The Power of the Mind

Back when I was working my ass off as a paid employee meeting extreme deadlines, some of us would work 12/7 until the jobs were out the door. This was private industry, not government, so the deadlines had to be met. Mostly because the jobs were government jobs. Ottawa is a government town. If the Nation's Capital were moved to . . . say, Vancouver, Ottawa would have nothing but a few archeologists wandering through empty buildings to cricket serenades. I suppose that's what kept me going, knowing that I was . . . What? That important? Whatever my motivation, it enabled me to continue without cessation until I'd fulfilled my responsibilities. And talk about a serotonin boost with all that stress and activity and coffee and excitement! Will we or won't we?

Within a day or so after a bout of this over-activity (essentially, at government year-end budget time), I would be half-dead with some waiting-in-the-wings cold or flu. This is where I'm at today. I have a bitchin' cold. I've even had to stuff my nostrils with tissues so I don't drip all over what I'm trying to do. Example: pulling down my undies to use the toilet (frequently, because I'm maxing on fluids) while trying not to snot on Kitty who always follows me in there. He likes to be close.

Why does this happen? The mind keeps the body working so well when we need it, that we don't come down with these pesky viruses until we tell it "Okay. Done."

It was a hard go again this year but I made it. Not that I've ever done it so can merely imagine what it would be like, but I feel like I've just run a marathon. And won. I am picturing those amazing Olympic marathon runners break through the tape at the end of their run and then collapse into the arms of handlers and doctors.

This too shall pass.

December 9, 2011

Koff, hack, snerf!

I'm feeling much better but still have symptoms of my cold or flu or whatever it is/was. I've been treating myself as though I love me by making myself rest under blankets while sipping herbal teas laced with lemon. I am fluffing my own pillows — no choice, I'm the only one who lives here except for Kitty. I do this in the manner of Kahlil Gibran who wrote "do everything as though it were for your beloved". What a Life's concept that is!

There's an old story about a man who went to Lourdes hoping to be cured of his affliction. What his affliction was I don't remember, nor does it matter. Concept, right? While he was in the crowd praying his heart out that he would receive a miracle — which, truth be told, didn't look too promising right then — he happened to notice a young boy who had a far worse condition than the man had. He was touched. He reached his thoughts out to the Being he was praying to and asked: "Please. Never mind me. Heal this boy. He needs it much more than I do." No rolling thunder or flashing lights or orchestras playing in the background, nor any Voice from Heaven but the man was cured instantly.

Why?

Love without any motivation but itself — and I mean Love with the capital letter, not the oh-I-just-love-chocolate kind of love, nor even the love one feels for one's spouse or sig-other (that's chemical) — is the most powerful tool we human beings possess and the most difficult to pull off.

December 13, 2011

G' morning

Yawn, stretch. I slept almost straight through last night for the first time in ages. Feels good. It was a beautiful sunny day yesterday and I ran a couple of errands first thing. I'm also waking up around 6:30 again and actually getting out of bed to start the day. (Last 14 days or so of The Bad Time, try as I might, I could NOT get myself out of bed at 6:00 anymore to turn on my light.) My energy has returned. Yay!

Now I gotta get crackin'. Have work to do. TONS of it!

December 19, 2011

Two-and-a-half More Sleeps

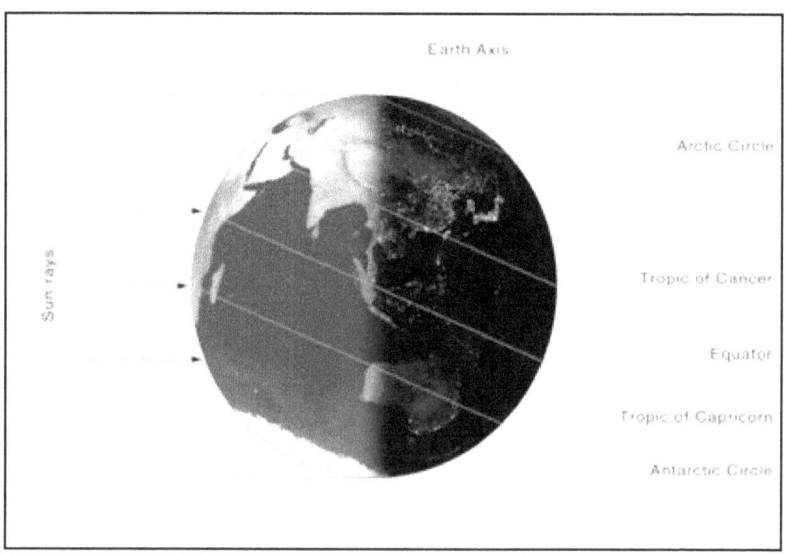

The Solstice approaches. This year it arrives December 22 at 12:30 AM.

What's the Solstice? That's the day the Earth's angle tips into a better (day length-wise) view of the Sun from our north-of-the-Equator section of the planet and the days begin to get longer. Australians, South Africans, and most South Americans are heading into their summer. http://en.wikipedia.org/wiki/Equator. The ancients have known about this since Pussy was a . . . well, I guess a sabre-tooth (http://en.wikipedia.org/wiki/Saber-toothed_cat): Stonehenge, the Maya calendar, the Valley of the Kings . . .

It's not so much the Earth tips, it's already at an angle (relative to the Sun). What happens results from the Earth's being off-kilter as it goes around the Sun — spin a toy top and you'll see what I mean if you picture the toy top spinning but leaning over to the right a bit. (For the technical among you, it tilts 23°26′.) It goes around the Sun counterclockwise, by the way. You'll see that as it goes around your pretend Sun, it will show its butt side when it passes around the right, then its non-butt side as it goes around the left. At its positions above or below the Sun, it will be exposed almost equally butt and non-butt. I can't find any public domain pix so you'll have to check this link out yourself: http://library.thinkquest.org/29033/begin/earthsunmoon.htm

The Winter Solstice is The Seasonally Depresseds' favourite day of the year. It's when the pressure starts to abate. The Summer Solstice (June 21 or 22) is when the days begin to shorten.

The January Blahs Folks

I'm aware that certain people find January/February extremely bad. It's something I haven't done any research on because it appears not to have anything to do with actual day-length but with the total length of the Too Damn Cold To Plant Anything Yet So I'm Stuck Eating Fucking Pickles And Jerky season. Yes? If any of you have difficulties during this time, please feel free to comment. Teach us!

Sang up a Lung on Saturday

Our choir had two Christmas carol gigs to do. The afternoon one was at a seniors' residence and the other was at a church in the evening. Great exercise for several body parts. Luciano Pavarotti called himself an athlete. During an interview he shared that his testicles jumped into his body when he hit the high notes. My husband at the time could sing and I asked him: "Hey. Is this bullshit? Or for real."

G says: "Let me check. Doh re mi fah sol la ti dooooooooooh. Yes. It's true. Cool. That's cool!" And off he went hitting the high notes for the rest of the week. I'm sure he demonstrated to his girlfriend, but I never got to see if it really was true or not. Took his word for it. If any of my readers are so inclined, check it out and let us know, okay?

January 16, 2012

Wow! Where has the time gone?

Been ages since I checked in. Hope all y'all are still alive and breathing with the same intellectual capacity (non-damaged brain tissue) y'all had before I last signed in.

What about that dirty bugger of a ship captain who bailed instead of going down with the ship, eh? Where have our once-noble ethics disappeared to?

February 26, 2012

Still here

I took most of November off as it seemed like the best way to handle this year's battle. This left me 30 days behind in my work, though. I am almost caught up. Whew! And TG because I have some new clients. Things are looking good business-wise. Yay! Always nice when something gets better, huh?

My friend and I were talking last week over lunch about how people get to be famous and rich and successful, etc. It looks like it ISN'T luck, it's bloody hard work with only a dollop of so-called luck. For example, if you want to be a famous movie star, you can't get to be one by sitting at home watching movies on TV. You have to get out there. If you want to be in a specific up-coming movie, then you have to kinda be where you have the greatest opportunity of being noticed and subsequently hired. It's just like any job — except there are usually a LOT more candidates scrambling for fewer positions. You decrease the odds substantially by working harder at it.

Life only sucks if you let it. (I will try to remind myself that I said this when October 2012 comes around. lol)

March 26, 2012

Easter's coming up

Anybody bugged by Easter? Passover? And I'm talking suicidally like Christmas sometimes is. Yes? No?

I'm not. Except that next week (April 1 to 8) we (choir) have lots of gigs for Holy Week. Ha! The church gang sure as hell doesn't like you calling them "gigs", but they are, lol. Especially our head honcho (parish priest) who gives the impression that the only way to god is through making yourself (and everyone around you if you're the head priest) miserable. But he's From Away. He's a South American Catholic where they have different views from us folks (Christian or not) here in Ottawa. Us Ottawans have different views from the folks who grew up [got programmed] in China, in Japan, in South Africa, in Israel, in Arabi al Saudi, in Alberta (cowboys), in Ireland (Christians but divided into further subgroups), Hawaii, New Zealand Aboriginals, Western Canada Aboriginals, Eastern Canada Aboriginals, Italians [north/south/central], the French, the Russians (how big is Russia? How many Thought Groups live there?) . . . Get my drift?

I have something to run by you guys.

One of the chicas in the choir (alto, so on the far side of the group from me) had a brother who got written up by the cops as a suicide about a year and a half ago. He was a druggie. His own guns were elsewhere and the gun that killed him was not his own. She's Catholic. If you're Catholic — so the story goes — and you kill yourself, you go directly to Hell, you do not pass GO. She is having such a bad time dealing with this that she's now a basket case. Her husband hasn't gotten laid for . . . Well. Let's not get too personal, okay?

How could I deal with this? Do I tell her that even though he killed himself and he's in Hell that life is marvy for her and her daughter and son and husband and other relatives? Do I support her in her belief that "others" killed him even though the cops don't agree with that?

See? What I'm trying to say here is that "religion" can fuck your head up so BAD that it can destroy you.

No matter who she goes to for comfort in the Catholic church, they will all tell her that her brother went to Hell for committing suicide and she will never see him again unless she goes to Hell too. How fucking stupid is that? If she goes to the cops, they'll tell her "yeah, he offed himself so like what's your problem? Lots of druggies do that." What can she do? Where can she go (in her mind) for comfort? Is it enough that every time I see her (practices and on Sundays) that I give her a pat on the arm or a hug to let her know that she's important to me?

See how you can really, really fuck up those who love you if you off yourself? You think it's all about you and wanting to get away from it all and you can't take it anymore and blabbedy bla . . . But what I learned from this woman is that it's damn near the meanest mother-fucking thing you can do to a relative or to somebody who loves you. OK. OK. To somebody who SAYS they love you. Give me a break! Lots of people love you. You can be the most twisted individual in the solar system but trust me, somebody is going to be fucked up if you off yourself.

Yeah. It's true. When you off yourself you go to a really nasty place. But that nasty place is the same place you just tried to get away from but magnified. I won't back down on that theory. But really, do you have to bring people who give a shit (whether you believe it or not) along with you? That's not the least bit fair. Not at all.

May 4, 2012

May 4

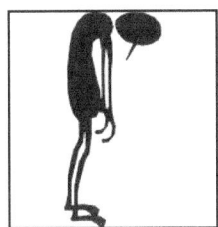

I just want to go away.

Leave all my stress-shits behind.

The list is long. I shan't bore you with any of it.

June 19, 2012

I'm in trouble ...

They cut me off my person who's been visiting once a week for over 6 years. Different person. Same concept. They've helped me ENORMOUSLY. I was rarely suicidal anymore.

But shit! They cut me off the help! It's not even June 21 (when the days start to get shorter) and I'm already suicidal. It's like: "Ah, the oxygen has worked for you. Excellent. Well we'll just learn from that and take your oxygen and give it to somebody else who needs it. There are a lot of people in line behind you."

Too bad, so sad, we need to give the oxygen to the next person in line. You'll just have to do without as you look so robust and healthy now. Eh? What's that? Do I hear a cough, cough, gag and some rales [rales = the death rattle] there?

Dalton McGuinty is a psychopath like most politicians and big-business peeps. He's behind the cuts.

May he rot in hell. I want to do a death-by-cop when I kill the fucker. I won't go alone!

June 20, 2012

Got mad yesterday and bitched

My "person" was allowed to come see me today.

I got angry and bitched yesterday afternoon and something got done. Wow. Open your mouth and say something instead of TAKING IT and things happen. What a concept.

Will keep you posted.

August 30, 2012

Gidday

September looms. Time to start writing again.

Got my person back but it sure has thrown me for a loop. But I shall work my way back again. Some good news coming up about my book, *A Girl Dog's Breakfast*. Will let y'all know. Also, some fun news about the project I'm working on currently.

Have kept myself busy — as required — but am going to take it easy this weekend. Just do stuff for moi and ignore everybody else. I'll try, anyway.

September 2, 2012

ha ha ha

Got caught up into this and that — actually, looking after some relatively newborn puppies — and happened to look up at the calendar today to see that it was already the second day of September. I was still in August! Proof positive that one can travel back in time if one is not paying attention.

Got to putting my Blog (this one) together for purposes of publication. Crowe Creations (crowecreations.ca) says they'll take it on like they did with A Girl Dog's Breakfast. Speaking of A Girl Dog's Breakfast, that will soon be available in print on Amazon.com. (It's already available on Kindle.) Will fill you in on particulars when that's accomplished. Having to read over my Blog from day 1 has knocked me out of the doldrums I was in.

Yay! Took my own advice!

After they had taken away My Person, I hit a downslide, as I mentioned in a June post. There was other stuff going on, too, like my mother was not well (still in hospital), and I started a new medication for my poor lungs back in May I think it was and it ended up that this new medication, although MARVELLOUS!, causes laryngitis (makes it a tad difficult to sing, yes?). But this, too, shall pass according to the research data.

I need to remind myself to fulfill the promise made on my website about what happens in Outer Darkness (i.e., after you die). In another post I'll get to it. Right now, I'm heading back to working on turning my Blog into book format.

Oh, yeah! My current project is a series of short screenplays. That's the exciting news I mentioned a few days ago. I plan to write about 10 or 11 of them and each takes about 10 minutes. (My Blog is already written, and is ongoing as we speak, so I don't feel guilty leaving my current project to give myself a break doing Something Different and work on the Blog.) At my writing group's Summer Social, I brought two of my finished screenplays and handed them out to various peeps and asked them if they'd like to take on a part. It was hilarious! Loads of fun.

For "Those Cohen Kids Again", in which Ben and Lauren Cohen and their babysitter's dog, Sparky, have to take on a pack of miniature 13th century Mongolians Warriors, the extras were simulating the sounds of arrows pinging and whistling, and battle horses neighing and even Sparky crying out when captured by the Mongol hoards.

"The Broken X Farm" is a darker piece. The "girls", Eva, Beatrice, Glenda, Mary and Stella (five show pigs who, Harv finds out much too late, speak English) object in their own way, complete with porcine humour, to the treatment of Harv's downtrodden wife, Amy. This played out with horror and humour as every actor got into it with snickering snorts every time the joker, Stella, opens her mouth.

We are hoping to get The Unkindest Cut on the shelves (Amazon.com) by spring. Watch for it.

September 12, 2012

I Tried Something New

. . . and it appears to be working.

In past years, I would turn on my light (http:// northern light technologies.com/) early in the morning and turn it off when I shut my drapes in the evening — earlier and earlier, of course. I have a wide ledge under my picture window. Great for plants. And my light!

Lately, I've been trying to force myself to get up as early as possible, like 5:00 AM if my eyes pop open at that time and I see the clock. Tired or not, I force myself up and start my literal morning (dawn) by turning on my light. (I have the luxury of working from home.) I leave it on until maybe 10:30 or 11:00 IF it's a nice bright day; otherwise, I leave it on.

Today, sunset will arrive at 7:21 PM here in Ottawa but, as you guys probably know, the sun's light starts to lose strength quite some time before that. So lately, I've been turning the light back on around 7:00 or so and turning it off at 8:30 exactly! Not one second before even though I can hardly see the TV and I'm getting spots in front of my eyes from the brightness — and this at 10 feet (3.048 m) away (I just measured it). I tuck my curtains behind it all the while mindful of a lamp touching cloth! I have the SADelite which is . . . Well, here's a photo of one:

I don't sit this close to it because I am able to have it on most of the day, but if you have to go to work or school or whatever, then you use it like this for about 30 minutes. Highly recommended and not just by me. Other people who have used it say that it's their saving grace, too. (The documentation says that people with blue eyes are more sensitive to it so need less time or might wish to keep it farther away. My eyes are green.)

Am feeling better — normal! — even this far into September this year. We'll see if this remains to be the case on October 26.

September 16, 2012

A Girl Dog's Breakfast

Here's the link to the Kindle version:
http://www.amazon.com/A-Girl-Dogs-Breakfast-ebook/dp/B007JN4KCK

And the link to the paperback: http://www.amazon.com/Girl-Dogs-Breakfast-Christina-Crowe/dp/1479214507/ref=sr_1_2?s=books&ie=UTF8&qid=1347821839&sr=1-2&keywords=a+girl+dog%27s+breakfast

September 17, 2012

Holy smokes!

I'm still doing very well and this deep into September. Interesting. I think it must have to do with forcing myself to keep the light on until 8:30 PM. I'm in my regular good mood. Cool and oh, so very welcome!

A friend suggested L-Theanine which is a mood enhancer thingey developed by the Japanese many years ago. It's derived from green tea. I am always paranoid about trying this kind of stuff. I know some people who tell me they've "developed" this "really great thing" that they use . . . Yeah. When I was in the Psych Ward I met some of them . . . There are always well-meaning peeps out there. We have to be careful. Our brain chemistry and our brain make-up isn't like everybody else's. We Suicidal Depressive have those extra receptors, right? You remember I told you that? Be careful.

However, if you want to check it out, here it is on Wikipedia: http://en.wikipedia.org/wiki/Theanine

I took a 125 mg tab yesterday. I didn't explode or anything. I didn't die. I'm going to wait until October 26 when the Bad Time usually kicks in and I'll try it then. Will certainly let yaz know.

September 21, 2012

Interesting Link

Check this out for some great ideas on how to relieve stress:

http://www.realage.com/mood-stress/easy-stress-busters-that-really-work?eid=1010665596&memberid=50181327

I just tried the last one — the breathing — and I feel better already!

October 5, 2012

So far so good!

Stretching my day out with the SADelite: ttp://www.northernligh techologies.ca/ and I am having very good results.

To reiterate:

I try to wake up around 5:00 or 6:00 AM — whether I want to or not! — and turn on the light. If it's a sunny day, I turn it off around 11:00 AM or so. It goes back on about half an hour before the sun goes down. (There's a subtle change in the sun's intensity about that time and we SADs can sense it.) Then I leave it on until 8:30 PM. No later, or I won't be able to sleep with that extra rush of serotonin and dopamine. The stuff we need. What it does is tell my system that we're still in early August so my body pumps out the chemicals I need.

As I said previously, I don't have this light glaring into my face that whole time. I work from home so have the SADelite on the picture window sill, like real sunlight would stream in. The evening stint is a bit different because when I watch TV, the light is shining right into my face from about 8 feet away. I have to hold the remote at a different angle to change channels or adjust the sound.

A friend told me about L-Theanine and I have tried it. I don't want to skew the experiment results so am not going to use it regularly until I know for sure that the new light regimen is causing my lighter mood.

Good news. That usual Guilt Cloud that starts hovering around starting in September, is amazingly absent this year. So far so good.

October 10, 2012

Still Doing OK

And I even had the funeral of a close family member to attend on the weekend.

I think The Bad Time is actually here because I have The Stupids, I'm tired, I ache, I am wanting to sleep a lot, and I don't feel very enthusiastic about much of anything, but blessedly, I don't have my Guilt Cloud following me around this year. Alle-fuckin'-luiah!

Will keep you posted.

October 12, 2012

Yawn! Stretch

This business of getting up in the middle of the night really sucks but the results are amazing.

I can't believe that the Guilt Cloud isn't following me around this year. I'm doing several different things:

I'm up at 5:30 or 6:00 AM to turn on my day (http://www.nor thernlighttechnologies.ca/#!__products/sadelite).

If it's sunny, I turn it off around 11:00 AM; if cloudy, I leave it on.

This is the different thing: I turn it on about a half hour before sunset (calendar here: http://www.sunrisesunset.com/) and leave it on until 8:30 even though it is shining right into my eyes when I'm trying to watch TV. I actually can't wait until 8:30 comes! But I am diligent about it.

I'm taking hormone replacements (estradiol). Research tells me it can boost mood. The literature tells me there are all kinds of precautions go along with this stuff. Hormone replacement can work for males, too (testosterone, in their case, of course), but men have to be very careful about dosages, etc., too, as it can cause a number of things including heart attacks and cancer. Neither of these should be a belly-up-to-the-pharmacy-counter pig-out. Doctor prescription and doctor monitoring only for any of these medications.

I've decided to continue with the L-Theanine (125 mg x 2/morning). I'll maybe remove it when I'm deep into The Bad Time (mid-November) to see if my Guilt Cloud suddenly floats in to besiege me. If it does (float in), then I'll know that the L-Theanine is helping keep it at bay. But maybe I'll wait until next year — or some week in the summer that has several dark days in a row. These affect me, too.

I've bumped up my B12 a notch, too. I'll be taking 250 until December 1. December 1 is when the Guilt Cloud goes away. It will be interesting to see this year, if all my aches and pains disappear at that time, too. I never paid much attention to that. The Guilt Cloud is what I want to escape from as it appears to be what produces that feeling of . . . being nothing of value.

Many people think that depression has to do with sadness. We Depressives know that's not true. But a really hearty laugh can produce oodles of serotonin so the opposite of sad can help us a lot.

So far so good. Yay!

October 21, 2012

Hot damn!

Talk about being in a bitchy mood! Woke up this morning on the wrong side of the bed for sure. Slept in until after 7:00 so maybe that had something to do with it? Have been sleeping very well though. That's a change from the usual at this time of year.

Anger > Guilt > Depression > Anger > Guilt > Depression > bla bla

I'm better now though because I went to choir this morning. We practise for an hour before we sing so that ends up to be pretty much two hours of singing. And singing is exercise! I keep forgetting that it's exercise. And often feel GUILTY when those in the know (medical peeps) tell me I should exercise and I forget to mention that I exercise with singing for two hours a shot, twice a week.

I should (there's that guilt-inducing word "should" again) exercise for myself anyway, but also, exercise gets the old serotonin running so I should for that reason, too. We need all the serotonin we can get. . . . in ways that don't put ourselves in danger with risky behaviour, right?

So far so good even this late into October otherwise. The Guilt Cloud is still absent. Yay!

Ah, and I learned how to say so far so good in Italian: "Fino au hora, tutto bene." :-D

Laughing is one of the best serotonin producers though. So seek out what makes you laugh and do it.

October 25, 2012

Interesting . . .

My sister-in-law, who's a nurse, reminded me that I should be doing exercises. Exercising boosts the serotonin levels. That's what we Depressives need.

Yeah, yeah. I knew that, but I tend to "forget" all the time that it would be a great help. After I do exercise, I feel so much better about myself and about everything, that I tell myself to keep it up. But I never exercised when I was growing up so it was never on my daily bucket list. It wasn't the trend back then. Besides, I was always extremely active, overly skinny and I swear I practically ran everywhere. At least I walked fast. I'm tall so have long legs and all my friends used to complain. (Sorry about that, guys.) So, unfortunately, exercise is not now one of my priorities either. I must change that brain pattern and forge new pathways in there to make me want to exercise. It's doable. Yes, you can forge new pathways in your brain. http://www.sciencedaily.com/releases/2009/11/091117161118.htm

I do have a list of exercises that I more or less "designed" myself. I'd forgotten about them (gee, I wonder why, eh?) even though I have pieces of paper stuck in several places around the apartment. They're stretches more than anything else. See, I sit at the computer working most of the time and hate taking time away from my work as I want to get the jobs done and out of the way. (Excuses, excuses!)

These are kinda fun and don't take long. I can do pretty much all of these while the coffee is running through.

1. knee bends (feet flat) x 10
2. heel lifts x 10
3. pushaways (body straight) x 10
4. foot squishes (hip rotations) x 10
5. can lifts (left) x 10
6. can lifts (right) x 10
7. can lifts (front) x 10
8. door twists (left, right) x 5
9. door hangs (head up) x 10

My kitchen counter has a turn in it. I stand in the vee of the turn and hold onto the counter (standing straight up) while I bend my knees as low as I can — with my feet slightly apart and flat on the floor — 10 times.

Standing straight up, I do the heel lifts as high as I can in that same spot.

The "pushaways" are exactly that. While I hold onto the rim of the sink/counter and with my body straight, I do the equivalent of pushups, but they are pushaways from the sink. I started doing them up close to the sink but am gradually getting my feet farther and farther back. I use my yoga mat to ensure that my feet don't slip out and I end up knocking my teeth out on the counter. That WOULD be counteractive to reducing one's depression, wouldn't it?

The foot squishes I just started doing yesterday because when I was waiting at the bus stop a couple of days ago, an elderly Chinese woman went up to the concrete porch behind us, grabbed the bottom of two railings, jammed one foot FLAT against the porch at street level (heel touching the sidewalk, toes up — Ouch?), and with both legs straight and body straight, leaned her body forward and backward several times. You can't do this without swivelling your hips. (Picture her legs being in an upside-down vee from the hips.) I tried it yesterday — can't get my foot flat against the bottom of the counter yet, of course! — but what a workout it gives to your hip sockets! That should scrape off some of the arthritic deposits. Yes?

Can lifts: Start with a small can — canned cat food (354 gram size) has a nice weight to it — and gradually work your way up to using a bag of beans or a package of spaghetti or whatever's handy that will fit comfortably in your hand. (You don't want a big can of tomatoes to slip out of your hand and bonk you on the head.) Holding the can loosely in your left hand with your arm hanging down, either lift it straight up as far as you can, or you can stretch it out to the side in an arc. The former is much easier. You could graduate to the harder method later.

Then do the same with your right arm.

For the front can lifts, hold the can with both hands and either go straight up (to start) or out and up once you get stronger. This is the one I do with my cat sometimes. Seriously. He doesn't like it so goes all stiff which makes me have to work harder. And it makes me laugh at the same time which is good for that extra bit of serotonin. My other cat was a former show kitty so loved being lifted up in the air and back down.

For the door twists, I put one arm straight out to the left and in front of a door jam, the other behind the door jam and push as far as I can while I try to look behind myself. Then I switch to back and front of the door jam. I do this once per side, 5 times. Hurts like a bugger when you start out but you find yourself gradually being able to see farther and farther behind you. There's a yoga position similar to this but this is a standing twist.

I like the door hangs because they seem to quiet all my screaming muscles after all the other twisting. I am able to reach the top frame of my door, so I hook my fingers over that. If you can't reach the top of the door frame, then you might consider installing a bar — not that kind of bar, silly! — I mean like a shower bar. But don't do this in the shower as shower bars don't support enough weight if you happen to slip. You could accidentally kill yourself. How embarrassing would that be? I'll explain the door hangs then provide an alternative for those of you who can't reach the lip. Feet apart to hip level, and with fingers hooked over the frame, look up and lean forward as far as you can but keep your eyes looking at the top of the frame. This will make you stretch your neck backwards as your body goes forward. Do this slowly and hold the forward position. Breathe out when you lean forward and in when you lean back.

Alternative. You can do this with your hands raised and flat against a wall and your feet about the length of one of your feet back from the wall, but you will risk banging your chin against the wall once you get going and you can't really lean far enough forward.

Try those and let me know if they work for you or not.

October 28, 2012

Must be doing something right

October 26 has been The Magic Number for me — or the un-magic number maybe — for years and years. It seemed to be the day when the Guilt Cloud (and all its nasty little friends) poured down on me with hurricane strength and wouldn't leave until December 1.

Nothing happened this time. It's already October 28 and I'm still doing OK.

I'm sure it's the light regimen I've been on: keeping my SADelite on until 8:30 PM no matter what. Sometimes I can hardly stay awake that long because I am tired and wanting to sleep. Maybe it's the combination of the boost of Vitamin B12 or the L-

Theanine. Maybe the hormone therapy? Whatever it is, I am soooo glad it's working. And I'm not going to mess with anything until after the Winter Solstice. The Pagans had wisdom after all. They celebrated the Winter Solstice. Is that to celebrate having survived the Dark Time once again? The First Nations of Canada celebrate the solstices, too.

I'm doing great mentally, but am noticing easy fatigue; a desire to sleep, sleep, sleep; a profound stupidity ("The Stupids" I call it); and aches and pains which were most likely always there before but my main concern was with not killing myself because of the Guilt Cloud.

It's getting harder and harder to get up at 5:30–6:00 (I go to bed at 9 PM so what's my problem?) but I must force myself to do it so I can get my day(light) started. The sun is not rising until 7:30 and later so my light is all I have until then. Really weird to see it so dark outside; the songbirds have already fucked off down south so it's quiet, too. The leaves are still on the trees here though and they're a bright, warm yellow like the sun and the leaves that have fallen are a carpet that brightens the eye of the beholder. Some of the trees are only bare branches reaching their fingers to the sky, but even they have a life about them. I know that their edges and ends hold the promise of spring but they need that special sleep first. Soon, we'll get that inevitable blast of wind that will take everything down.

Until then, I'll enjoy it.

Hang in there. I'm trying to give you as much information as possible in the most sincere hope that it will help you find a trick or two that will hold off your Black Dogs, or throw a rope into your Pit so you can climb out. I am in no way "cured", but so far so good (fino au hora, multo bene) this year. One day at a time, right?

November 3, 2012

And the beat goes on!

I'm still doing great. Amazing. Except for the aches and fatigue and The Stupids, that is, but I can deal with those — only 28 days to go until December 1. Although . . . Maybe these symptoms will last until December 21 when the days start to get longer. I never made note of these symptoms before, never paid much attention to them, so we shall see.

Next Hurdle: The Dreaded Time Change

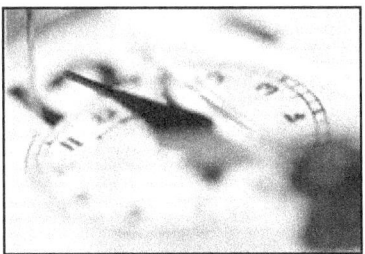

This always used to throw me for a huge loop. I would be just starting to adjust to late October's gradual slide, minute by minute, into darkness and be actually handling it quite well, when ka-boom, I'd be knocked off kilter by a whole hour. I have noticed in the past few years, since they changed the date of The Dreaded Time Change, that it wasn't as severe a blow.

We shall see what the change does this year when I am doing so well.

Sleepy, Though

I find I am sleeping in despite my wishes not to. It was 8:30 when I finally dragged myself out of bed this morning to turn on my SADelite. Wow. I woke at 4:30 and again at just before 5:00 but said to myself: "Just a minute or so longer and I'll get up at 5:30. That'll be good."

But my internal clock must have malfunctioned — or else I got into a good dream? — but next thing I knew, it was 8:30 and the cat was yelling at me. That just reminded me of what my mother used to say to us kids: "C'mon. Get up. Get outside and get some of the stink blown off ya." That still makes me laugh.

November 5, 2012

I'm OK. I'm OK.

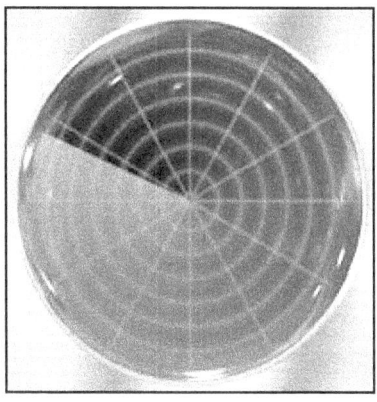

Hardly a blip on the radar at all. But there was a blip.

Had some overtime work to do on Friday night so didn't have as much of a day off as I'd hoped. Saturday was busy, too. And Sunday morning and, and . . .

By Sunday evening when I lay down to watch some TV (and read during the commercials), I couldn't keep my eyes open so must have slept for a good hour or more. Deeply! I've already mentioned that I have my SADelite on the window sill and hang the draperies around behind it until 8:30, but when we are sleeping that deeply, the light somehow doesn't get through the same.

When I woke up there was a pretty decent movie on (the kind I like, at least) and I started watching it. I don't know what triggered it, but a little cloud of Guilt drifted in and I started with that same old feeling of being "bad" and "hated" and "no good fer nuthin' but fertilizer and even then maybe not".

I was quite disappointed while I tried to convince myself that this was not true, that I had probably messed things up by sleeping. "They" do advise against sleeping during the day (fake day or not) if you have problems with seasonal depression.

"Dammit," I thought. "How can I get out of this pickle?"

I stared right at the light for about five minutes then went surfing for the Comedy channel on TV. Luckily I found an hour's worth of stand-up comedy then two half-hour slots of a show called "lol". By the end of those two hours, I was laughing my head off and feeling great again. In fact, it only took about five minutes into the stand-up show for that awful mood to lift.

Looks like we CAN get our serotonin flowing without doing anything dangerous to ourselves or harmful to others (like risky sex or starting a fight in a biker bar).

November 7, 2012

Still OK

Like I said, a couple of minor blips on the Pit/Black Dogs radar but otherwise, things are totally peachie! I can't believe it.

My friend told me yesterday: "Get a light, get a life." That's about the size of it. Wow.

Try it, guys. Please. Just TRY IT!

November 9, 2012

No Info on SAD South of the Equator

I did some research to see if folks south of the Equator had seasonal depression in their autumn and winter, too. There doesn't seem to be any data — although I did find this link: http://www.strisik.com/ss/pubs/sad_part_1.htm which is a good check-list for those of you who are wondering if you fit.

Looks like people in New Zealand, Chile and Argentina have Latitude 45 (like Ottawa here) pass through the country. They'll be in their spring now, heading into summer. I wonder if any of them have problems with seasonal depression . . .

Most of what is south of the 45 and up Latitudes is Antarctica. Did you ever have a look at that thing on a map? It is absolutely HUGE! You could fit almost everything but Russia into it.

November 14, 2012

I Learned Something!

I belong to a writing group and last night they had a mini-workshop on Blogging. It's not that I'm doing all that much wrong, there's just a lot of stuff I haven't been doing at all. Mostly because of my background (and other reasons) I tend to be a little more cautious than most about giving out personal information. And no, I'm not on the run from the Law or anything.

Don't forget the "risk" part of the symptoms of depression. I've met some baddies in my life — for example, I was stalked for over a year by a crazy Palestinian on drugs so am extra diligent by nature now. And that was a long time ago.

I'm not saying anything against him as a Palestinian — the last thing I am is a racist — it's just that he was a Palestinian terrorist back in the day (late 70s), ex-PLO as a matter of fact and had belonged (or so he said) to one of those groups that had a day in it — not a month like the Black September group, a day. (Can't remember either the English or the Arabic word anymore. I think it was one of those things that your Little Voice tells you to forget as soon as you hear it?) So he knew how to scare people. He'd been trained.

Lucky, Lucky, Lucky

See how lucky I am to be still alive? This guy was the stereotypical abuser: pathologically jealous, "nobody will ever love you the way I do baby" [TG for that!], slapping me around, scaring me, isolating, berating. It was mostly the drugs. (Or so I tell myself. More about the Right Man — and I don't mean Mister Right! — in a future post.) Sad. He was a very intelligent man. Damaged by history. I loved him a lot but.

One time we went to a relative's house and he opened the door off the kitchen into the porch which was full of guns lined up against the wall on shelves. I quickly turned away but as you must know, what has been seen can't be unseen.

He called out my name and when I turned back, he was pointing one of the guns (Uzi?) right at my face. He pulled the trigger. He laughed. He put the gun back.

See how lucky I am to be still alive?

November 17, 2012

Two Nights Ago . . .

Slept well last night but two nights ago I tossed and turned most of the night. Six AM came much too quickly.

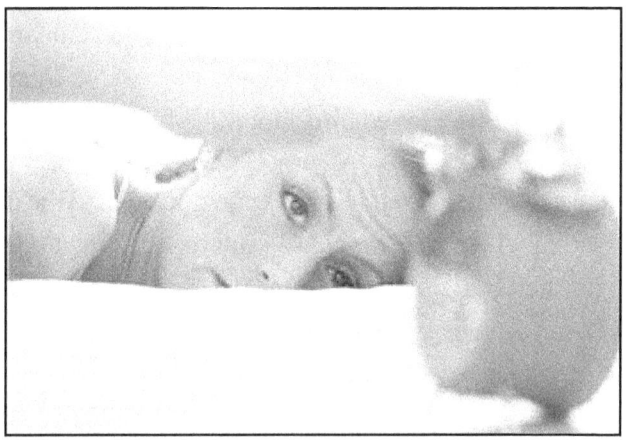

Made up for it last night but didn't wake up until after 7 AM this morning. But I'm here now, "alive and breathing".

During the night (two nights ago), I had "Thoughts" going through my head like I sometimes do during The Bad Time or even when I'm under stress normally. I think this is what kept me awake — plus several cups of green tea, the latter which I always tell myself never to do again at bedtime unless it actually says decaf on the bag. (It's the rebel in me. The risk-taker. Right?)

The Thoughts are of something current going on. Something that's making me look like the Wicked Witch of the West although I'm not at all. I've resigned from a position that was taking up ~25% of my life. It was something I really enjoyed doing, but I had to set my clients (and myself) aside to accommodate it. Then my client based workload increased as did my Writing To Do Piles so I had to make a decision. The volunteering job that I'd been doing for over six years now had to go.

Fine and dandy. I have no regrets . . .

. . . except that I am being looked upon as somebody who has run off to some island in the Caribbean with the company funds. "Where are all the articles you have stashed away for the next five or six publications?"

"There ain't none, honey child! I have to scramble for those every single issue! They don't just drop in on my head when the fairies fly over. That's why I resigned the position. Six years of scrambling for six issues a year have taken their toll."

I have enjoyed it. Made connections. Increased my clientele. Am looked upon with awe by some (that's so cute!). And am nit-picked half to death from another corner but I know how to roll with the punches. Mommy Dearest taught me well.

Triggers The Cycle

For me, it is distressful to be mis-perceived. If I'm going to be perfectly honest, I have to say that it actually pisses me off to the nth degree. Gives me sleepless nights. Sends me into an Anger -> Guilt -> Depression cycle I get so filled with rage.

And yes, there are deep-rooted reasons (of which I am fully aware) for my being a tad(?) more sensitive in that area that another might be. Perhaps for a future post?

What shall I title it: "How My Little Sister Tried to Steal My Personality because She Had None of her Own [schizophrenia? psychopathy? sociopathy? who knows?] but She Was such a Bitch when She Was Me that She Made Everybody Run away Screaming from Me, Too"?

November 21, 2012

A Weekend in the Bush

What a wonderful area. Mostly cedars and rocks there so I love it. Rejuvenates the soul.

This is one of the Weimaraner gals trotting away. The other guys

I dog-sit, if you recall, are Cavalier King Charles Spaniels. Huge difference in energy levels!

Spent last weekend there.

Am still doing really well for its being November 21! Ten days to go until December 1. I will continue to maintain my light regimen — my body/mind thinks we're in August so I don't want to get jet lag. ha

Managed to get through two big chunks of jobs today. It's wonderful not having that other one hanging over my head anymore. I feel like a new woman. Not really.

(This reminds me of an old, old joke where a woman says, "I am doing so well lately, I feel like a new man." hee hee)

November 22, 2012

Our Men & Women in the Forces

At this time of year, we think of our own families and friends. However, many military personnel serving in overseas posts are far away from family or, possibly don't have family. Whether one supports or opposes military service, these folks are still alone.

So, an item for the newsletter ... or perhaps a link from your website ... would allow cards and letters to be sent.

1) Address envelopes to:

"Any Canadian Forces Member"

2) A list of the mailing addresses for the various overseas postings can be found at the following website. Click on the location for a full address:

http://www.forces.gc.ca/site/commun/message/addresses-eng.asp

November 23, 2012

Impromptu Test Proves Something

I went somewhere yesterday so was without my SADelite from around 4 PM to bedtime.

And had a restless night until I realized what was going on and told myself to shut up.

It wasn't a full-fledged Guilt Cloud that floated in during a restless night, but more like a puff of You're Soooo Bad and Evil Because . . . I can't even remember this morning what the "becauses" were but as soon as I told myself to stop doing that and went instead to my little trick of trying to spend a billion dollars, I managed to sleep well until this morning.

Was up at 5:30 AM, SADelite on, and I feel quite upbeat this morning. Amazing how much good the extra day length, however phony, is helping. This is proof. Undeniable proof. Nothing else was altered, meaning the B12, L-Theanine, and other supplements. Only the day length.

Come December 1 (8 days to go), I think I'll gradually make my SADelite day get shorter (at the end), let's say by five minutes a day maybe, until December 21 — that wonderful Winter Solstice when the days start getting longer again. I wonder when my fake day length and the actual day length will coincide. I'll check that out and get back with the info.

[It would be January 24, 2013, so maybe I'll make the change more slowly, like 2 minutes a day.]

November 28, 2012

3 Days to Go

I guess I can safely say that I made it through another November.
Yay!

This is what I'm doing right now:

Lovely. Peaceful. Envy-producing . . . Yes?

Do not be deceived. It's usually like this:

There's a squirrel in the back yard.

I really enjoy getting my dog fixes.

November 30, 2012

Nov 30, Nov 30! I am so excited!

Holy poopee doodies! I have like . . . [calculate, calculate] . . . about 4 hours left until December 1.

Yay.

I KNOW I have made it through another November. woohoo woopee-doo

OK.

So now what do I need to do?

I have figured out how to deal with my own seasonal depression so it is incumbent upon me to do a shit load of research to find out how I can help OTHERS deal with their particular depression.

So . . . guys . . . Put away the pills, the nooses, the maps to the bridges that are good to jump offa — (Where I grew up there was a bridge that peeps jumped off. It wasn't even deep water there. Can't understand why . . . But when I wasn't even in my Bad Time and if I went to that bridge, I would have this terrible urge to leap off it. Shit-la-merde! Special Bridge, eh? I will try to address that in future posts. I know, I know. I already owe you guys one about Out Darkness and why you DO NOT wanna go there.)

I'm home from my dog gigs for quite a while now so will try my best to fit that in among my other responsibilities . . .

December 2, 2012

Made it!

Yay.

Not much time to write as I have to go sing. But just wanted to let you know that the fog has lifted — whatever fog was there this year. Amazing. I'm already off the L-Theanine and will lower my B12 dosage back to what my doc said I should be taking. Didn't boost it by much and checked MANY sources on the Internet as to recommended dosages.

Vitamins: Read the Label

Vitamins are not innocent of causing problems. For instance, "they" are saying now that too much calcium can cause heart problems. And here's a link to what a person can overdose on vitamin-wise:

http://chemo.net/newpage35.htm

So just tell your mom that too much spinach (too much iron, too much calcium) can kill you. But then you'd better duck or your mother will be worse than spinach for you.

December 5, 2012

Oh. It's Wednesday. Yes.

Seems I've been posting on Wednesdays and Fridays but usually early in the AM.

Bad me, today. I got up at 5:30 and started — almost immediately — working on Volume 2 (the design of) of The Creation of the Black Russian Terrier, Moscow: The Karabashka Group. Well, to you it might sound kinda boring but there are a lot of dog peeps out there who LOVE this shit. (Me is one of them.)

See the thing is, Stalin and Beria wanted a specifically Russian dog that would eat what they considered to be The Bad Guys. They already had the Caucasian Ovcharka (see below comparing a pissed off Grizzly with a pissed off Caucasian Ovcharka):

Easy to believe that the dog and the bear are closely related, eh?

Donald B. Anderson has been working on this book (now a series of 8 volumes and maybe more) for I think he said about 8 years now. Vol. 1 is available at Amazon.com.:

http://www.amazon.com/Creation-Black-Russian-Terrier-KGBeast/dp/148025763X/ref=sr_1_1?s=books&ie=UTF8&qid=1354742475&sr=1-1&keywords=the+creation+of+the+black+russian+terrier

You know, sometimes when I think I've had a bad day I think of the guys in the Russian gulags (prisons) who have to deal with these Caucasian Ovcharkas all the time. Last year I managed to catch a program about the poor schmucks and nearly dirtied my undies when I saw just how BIG those flipping dogs are! I emailed Don immediately to say "Holy shit, man! Those suckers are mean!"

Here's another shot of how tall they are (but this is the South Asian Ovcharka and it's with its Mommy so likes her):

I worked hard today and around 1:00 PM or so, I felt like a combination of the Grizzly and Mr. Personality up there. But I got over it.

December 7, 2012

You Know, It's Funny But . . .

Since I resigned from that volunteer position I told you about in my November 17 post, "Two Nights Ago", my life has really taken a turn for the better. There is no longer that invisible Thing putting pressure on my shoulders. I've actually been able to put out two books for clients since then. One of them was a put-it-together-over-a-weekend designed one for Dorothee Komangapik which is an absolute total delight. I recommend it for "kids" of all ages.

There's nothing like the rush of doing something that makes another person's face — whole body! — light up with joy. I call myself a midwife with this book editing/design stuff. When you see what happens when the person first holds their book in their hand . . . Wow.

It's available on Amazon.com: http://www.amazon.com/Small-Household-Dorothee-Komangapik/dp/1481002244/ref=sr_1_1?s=books&ie=UTF8&qid=1354907398&sr=1-1&keywords=the+small+household

It's also available on Amazon.com as a Kindle book. The Kindle version is FREE Saturday, December 22 and again on Saturday, February 9 so there are no excuses for not downloading it, are there? (In case you aren't aware, you can download Kindle books onto your PC. There's a link on Amazon.com for that.)

December 8, 2012

Stressed to the Max?

Some good tips here:

http://www.realage.com/soothe-stress/burnt-out-and-exhausted-from-work-stress-or-job-hunting-how-to-recharge?eid=1010673689&memberid=50181327

Each day following my resignation from that volunteer gig, I wake up feeling less stressed and I see that "cutting back" is listed. Knowing I did something right adds to that feel-good atmosphere which tends to grow like The Blob.

http://www.imdb.com/title/tt0051418/

This was Steve McQueen's first role, btw, for those history buffs among you. (He was called "Steven" McQueen back then.)

December 13, 2012

Missed Yesterday's Post

Appears my immune system got compromised and I ended up with a dilly of a cold that started on Tuesday. I shall not whine — even though I want to — but instead will keep this short. But I do have excuses.

Dealing with November (my Bad Time) is quite stressful even though this year I was spared the Guilt Cloud. But stressful, nonetheless. On the heels of that, I had a couple of dog-gigs in there that were more physical than usual. (My work demands hours of sitting at a computer so when I do physical work, I feel it!) Then back to the real world and oodles of choir practice for a concert on Saturday night which meant we were there from around 5 PM until 9:30 or so. Then back the next morning at 9 AM for practice and a big special Service.

All this in itself would not normally faze me too much except that I had to prepare for a routine test on Monday morning so was not allowed to eat anything all day Sunday and all of Monday morning. And I had to drink some stuff that sent my whole system into an uproar.

I slept on the couch last night from about 8 PM to 8 AM all propped up on pillows because my breathing — that would be my difficulty with breathing — was scaring me. Folks? If you don't smoke now, don't start. And if you do. Stop. I smoked for many, many years and now my lungs are fucked.

It's funny but when I'm in my Bad Time I think nothing of killing myself, but when I am not there, the thought of death terrifies me. Or, let me clarify that. It's not so much death that terrifies me although I don't like to wonder how I might go out, but it's that I have so much to do before I go.

Look at this!

And this is only part of it. The big pile is my projects. This doesn't even count the ones in my head that I haven't started on yet. (And The Unkindest Cut, a book of short creepy scripts slated for spring publication on Amazon.com, is on my coffee table. That's about an inch thick. I have lots to do before I shuffle off.

December 15, 2012

Yabut, There's No Chocolate!

Foods that Fight Depression

I know, I know. I've posted most of this before, but a refresher is always good.

http://www.realage.com/major-depression-mdd/mdd-food-and-depression?src=nl&dom=realage&list=tod&link=tod-bullet&ad=mdd&eid=1010674628&memberid=50181327

I eat most of this stuff and I mostly eat this stuff. Plus, my doctor has had me on B12 for a few years. (Good boy!) And Calcium and D too, of course because Mom has osteoporosis really bad. I have it to a certain extent now, too. I don't want to end up all curled over but probably will.

Food

What we take in foodwise affects us a lot more than we realize.

Last weekend, in preparation for my procedure, I had to eat Jello and apple juice and stuff like that. (O.J. makes my eczema break out.) The Jello pack stated proudly: NO SUGAR ADDED! Yay, I thought. Got it home only to discover that it has that fake sugar crap in it. Eating that stuff is like taking not-actually-poisonous poison and by that I mean that our system reacts to it like it's real sugar anyway so why not eat the real (organic) stuff than the chemically produced "imaginary" stuff. And besides, it's so overly sweet it's . . . gross.

I was also informed that I could eat/drink "broth" and other clear liquids. Well, even the proudly stated "LOW SODIUM" broths have lots of other crud in them. No wonder I got sick. Have a gander at the ingredients:

- water — OK, more than likely real H2O but you have to wonder if they just took it out of a tap somewhere or did it come from the Arctic (good, safe, non-polluted source) or maybe downstream from a nuclear station? . . .
- concentrated chicken broth — what the hell is "concentrated" chicken broth? When I make chicken broth it ends up so thick it's like a jelly so I guess that's "concentrated" but why use the term? Do they dehydrate it into a powder or something? Then sprinkle preservatives on it to keep it from going bad? What a thought!
- salt — the 3rd ingredient is SALT! I used to get major migraines and PMS enough to put me in danger of being a murder victim until a shrink told me to reduce my salt to minimal levels. This was in my late 30s early 40s. Guess what? It worked.

- flavour — how mysterious! "flavour". hmmm
- monosodium glutamate — Remember Robbie the Robot? "Danger! Danger!"
- yeast extract — you can extract stuff from yeast? Cool. And this "yeast extract" contains mustard oil. hmmm
- disodium inosinate — http://en.wikipedia.org/wiki/Disodium_inosinate Looks like this is an ingredient of monosodium glutamate, above. Double, double, toil and trouble.
- disodium guanylate — http://en.wikipedia.org/wiki/ Disodium_guanylate It says not to feed it to kids under 12 weeks of age, to asthmatics, and it can also cause gout. Let's see. I drank 2.7 litres of this shit in one day? Plus the fake sugar in the Jello. No wonder I got sick!
- dextrose — sugar
- citric acid — fake lemon juice
- chicken fat — chicken fat
- carrot juice extract — On the face of it I'll take their word for this one
- caramel colour — where do you get caramel colour from? Sugar and it appears a bunch of chemicals and maybe some salt, too?

I read ingredients like I were living with Lucrezia Borgia and had pissed her off somehow. If you find you have an afternoon free with nothing much to do someday, grab some packages off your shelves or out of your fridge or freezer and Google the ingredients. I shudder to think what might be in the fast foods you purchase over the counter that are not legally obliged to put ingredient labels on.

Just so you know I'm not some paranoid nut-case, I got into reading (studying) labels when I was into breeding dogs. All we'all were paranoid nut-cases about what we fed our precious little babbies. If the dog-food manufacturers poisoned our pets, we could just sue their asses off or spread the word and put the bastids out of business that way. We humans are not so lucky. We got that crap in EVERYTHING now. Sugar and salt lurk every-where undetected.

I'll try to remember to show you how to make chicken broth. Then after that, how to make the most amazing soup(s). Healthy broth! Healthy soup!

December 16, 2012

How to Make Really Healthy Broth (Part 1)

Here's how to make a really good healthy broth. What you need:

- shed
- special corrugated cardboard to use as a "fence"
- lots of newspapers
- shavings
- waterer
- feeder
- chick feed for the very young chick (if the pieces of feed are too large to go down the chick's gullet, they'll choke to death)
- thermometer
- about 5, day-old chicks
- time on your hands

Drive out to some small town/village in the boonies and find a

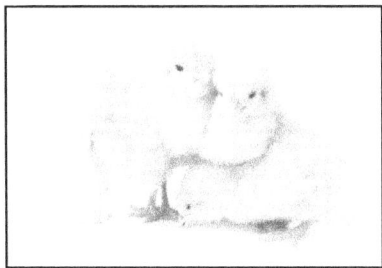

Co-op where they have information pamphlets; or you can download information from your government's Agricultural department. You will actually have to know about these Co-ops to purchase feed in the first place so this should not be a really terrible stretch.

Layer the shed floor with newspapers. Unroll the corrugated cardboard stuff to make a corral. Set the waterers and feeders down then spread out the shavings but not too deeply.

Get the environmental temperature — and especially the water — up to around 85 degrees F.

Then you may put the chicks in.

Ensure they know where the waterers are. Chicks are pretty smart about this. Turkeys are really stupid. You have to put marbles in the waterer so they head for the glitter and discover that water lieth there as well.

Do not feed for the first 24 hours. They MUST have water first. These guys just got born yesterday, right?

Check the chicks temperature-wise every few hours until they are about 2 weeks old.

Upgrade the feed and lower the temperature as they grow up and develop their feathers. Sort of like this:

When they have their feathers you can let them have access to the outdoors provided you have a very large fenced area with grass and nice bugs and probably a few Rottweilers running loose to keep them safe from neighbourhood dogs, cats, fishers, hawks, owls, turkey vultures (yes! they tried to get my guys once!) and Bylaw guys. Well, we were in the boonies so didn't need to worry about Bylaw guys, but if you live in the City . . .

When they are about 10 to 12 weeks old, build a kind of gallows thing and get some twine. Cut the twine into five equal pieces and make little nooses. Build a big bonfire and boil a garbage pail full of water over it.

Oh, but the night before you do this, go out there and thank them for their bodies that they will be giving to you the next morning.

You can give them a last little snack of savory, thyme and sage from your garden. They love that stuff and it kinda pre-flavours them.

Do this with respect. I joke about this but when I used to do it, I would go out there with my soul bared, and with nobody around, and I would actually aim my words at the spirits of the chickens. We raised a lot more than 5 at a time though, maybe 75-100.

I'd say — and feel a little silly while saying it, yes of course I did, but it is the Aboriginal way in Canada and elsewhere you know! — "OK, guys. Don't know which of you will be leaving tomorrow, but thank you. Your body will keep my body alive." And I'd actually cry because it was a special moment believe it or not. Try it some time.

Next time you are sitting down for a meal, don't thank God for it, look down. Look down at the peas, or the asparagus, or the fish and — I dare you not to shed a tear! — thank the vegetables or the creature on your plate for giving its life for you.

OK. Now YOU must do what our ancestors did in order to have you and moi actually HERE right now: Survive long enough to reproduce. I am going to throw out a theory about Neanderthal Man. I can see Mr Neander raising his stone axe over the neck of some poor captured rat. Mr. Neander is ready to do whatever necessary to feed Mrs. Neander and the kiddies during the Ice Age, back when veggies were scarce to non-existent. But Mrs. Neander stays his hand: "Oh, honey. But it's so CUUUTE!"

Carry on.

Grab the chickens and hang them upside down by one foot. Then take your little what they call a "pen knife", then one at a time, open a chicken's mouth and in one deft motion, almost simultaneously brain-stick it and cut its jugul—

No?

Well, then, you could go to your local market — NOT the supermarket! — and purchase 5 grain-fed and/or free-range already-dead ones. Around maybe 6 or 7 pounds each.

Or better yet, purchase five Kosher or Halal chickens. These guys have been treated just as kindly and with just as much respect as you would have if you'd been able to carry through with the business above about brain-sticking them, plunging them into the boiling water to make feather-removal easier, and then respectfully gutting them and cooling them quickly and then washing off any lingering poo (a.k.a., salmonella) before bagging them and putting them into your freezer for num-nums later.

Over the next few months, remove a chicken and cook it. It is preferable to roast them in the oven with summer savory, sage (easy on the sage), and thyme. If you cook them using different flavour principles (http://www.amazon.com/The-Flavor-Princi ple-Cookbook-Elisabeth-Rozin/dp/B0006C3YRI) from each other, the end result might be really gross.

When you cook these chickens go ahead and eat as much of them as you wish, but do NOT throw out the bones. It's all in the bones . . . Well mostly. Save the skin and the little bits of anything. Even the fat. (Don't worry, we'll deal with the fat later.) Put each carcass into its individual container/bag when you finish with each one, then pop the wee dear carcasses back into the freezer until you've used up all five.

Oh, yeah. Note. Don't save the dressing. It tends to "cloud the broth".

You can also start getting hog-ish about ANY bones that are left over from meals. Meals that YOU have cooked, that is. None of those chemical-laden pre-cooked grab-on-the-way-home-from work meals, please; but bones from restaurant doggie bags — like, restaurants with those things called "chefs"? — are OK to keep.

Then we will be off to Part 2 of how to make really healthy broth.

Shall I wait?

December 19, 2012

How to Make a Really Healthy Broth (Part 2)

What you need equipment-wise:

- stock pot. This is mine. The white thing beside it is a measuring cup of 1 cup.

- strainer or drainer or sieve or cheesecloth. These are a couple I have. Purists would probably use the cheesecloth and get a long stick and set this across a couple of chairs and let it drip through for many hours, but hey! This works for my soups. I am not making aspic for competition.
- 2 or 3 big containers. Pots are probably best; bowls are OK

but might be too tippy. You have to strain the bones and stuff out of the stock so you need something wide to accept the pouring; and large enough to hold all the stock for a little while.

- maybe three (?) plastic bags — with no holes in them! — to double/triple bag for putting the bones in for disposal.
- cutting knife/cutting board for chopping up onions and other stuf
- scissors (or good teeth to chew open some bags of frozen vegetables)

What you need soup-wise:

- dried beans. Probably about 2 cups of any of these: kidney beans, navy beans, pinto beans, great northern beans, pink beans, and/or cranberry beans. I usually have some of these beans on hand. They store well and easily. (I have a really good bean recipe, too, if you're OK with pork. Let me know and I'll post it.) You'll need to soak the beans overnight to remove the toxins (the substance in them that causes intestinal problems such as gas and bloating). Be sure to rinse them off well and toss the soaking water away.
- your 5 or so frozen chicken carcasses. (You may thaw them if you want but then you have to crowd up your refrigerator

while this is going on; also, if you thaw them, you are committed.)

- any other bones you have in your freezer that you have cooked yourself and that don't have any weird gravies or strong or conflicting-with-our-soup spices on them
- celery. Three stalks (whole) for making the stock; two or three stalks (sliced) when making the soup.
- carrots. Three carrots (whole) for making the stock; two carrots (scraped and sliced) for the soup.
- 3 cans of tomatoes. You can purchase these already pureed or puree them yourself but don't use them whole or even what they call "diced". You want smooth. Plum tomatoes have the best flavour. Make sure they are just plain tomatoes WITHOUT seasoning.
- pasta (optional). You know sometimes you are in a store and you see all these cute little pastas like stars or the alphabet or little indescribable thingeys and you wonder what they use them for? Now's your chance. We need maybe a cup of these.
- rice (optional)
- barley (optional) You'd opt for barley if you have quite a few extra beef or lamb bones that might tip the flavour scale from poultry to beef/lamb.
- lentils (optional) You can use these. They are "beans" but they don't soak like the ones above.
- 2 onions (medium to large)
- 2 medium garlic cloves. That is, NOT the whole thing. Just a couple of the sections. DO NOT PEEL THIS. It goes in whole.
- 8-10 whole cloves. You are going to stick these all over one

of the onions.

- 2-3 bags of frozen mixed vegetables. Please make sure these are not, for example, "Italian Vegetable Mix" with Italian seasonings, etc. We want a broad mix of broccoli, cauliflower, carrots, peas, beans, variously coloured peppers, etc. You can add vegetables "from away" (meaning vegetables that you never heard of before) but make sure they don't have their own seasonings added. Most do. Of course you should really have grown all these veggies in your own garden or at least have purchased them from a farmer's market, but hey! If wishes were horses . . .
- 20-30 little potatoes (optional). Those cute wee teeny ones. Wash them well. Do not peel but cut in half.
- parsley (tsp.)
- sage (1/2 tsp.)
- thyme (1/2 tsp.)
- savory (tsp.)
- 2 small bay leaves or one big one
- basil (tomatoes NEED basil) But do not overdo the addition of basil as it can be sickeningly sweetish. I'd say maybe 1/2-3/4 tsp.
- Cayenne pepper (1/8 tsp.) (at the end)
- Tabasco sauce (at the end) (shake, shake, shake, shake, shake STOP). (This is the secret ingredient. The five shakes of it.)

Do not put salt in until the end. Do not put pepper in until it is served.

Part 3 coming up . . .

December 20, 2012

How to Make a Really Healthy Soup (Part 3)

We are ready to go!

Put all your bones into the stock pot. Add cold water. Cold water. Add enough to cover. It's OK if a wing or leg is sticking up a bit as the carcasses will thaw and settle down later. If the level of water gets lower than you'd like, then add more cold water. Don't do this too often, though, you don't want to dilute it too much.

Crank the heat to high. It will take quite a while to get this up to a rolling boil but you have to keep an eye on it. Once it hits the magic temperature, it will get into a pretty robust bubbling. Let it boil for 10 minutes.

Do not stir at any time during this stage.

While you're waiting for this to get up to a boil you can prepare your carrots and celery and onion. Toss in your 1 or 2 bay leaves. Your two garlic thingeys.

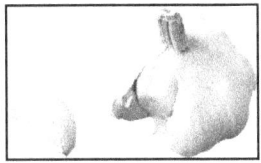

Peel one of the onions and stick 8-10 whole cloves into it.

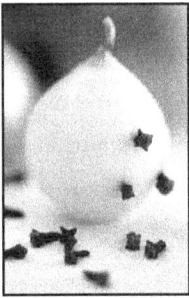

This can be hard on the thumb so improvise. Wash the carrots and celery and just snap them in half and pop them in. No need for presentation or artistic flare now as all these will be tossed away along with the used-up bones.

Turn down the heat so it will maintain a tad over a simmer. This means just a few bubbles in there. And keep this going for about 5 hours.

Stuff will float to the top. If you have a skimmer, you may skim this stuff off now but there's an easier way I'll tell you about later.

People who come to your door will sniff the air and say: "Hmm. Smells good. What are you cooking?"

You can throw them a mysterious smile and say, "Oh, that? Oh, nothing. Yet."

After about 5 hours have passed, turn it off and let it cool down a bit. This will obviously take quite a while. If it's winter and you have no critters in your neighbourhood, you can set it out on the porch overnight. You don't want it to freeze though, so use common sense. Or, put it in the fridge. You'll probably have to adjust your shelves in there to accommodate the pot.

Next day, you will see that there's a layer of "stuff" on the top of the cooled broth. Remove this with a skimmer or spoon. If your broth has turned out, the liquid below it will be almost like Jello. It will probably be clear, too. Very nice! Bravo!

Next step, with or without gloves — if without gloves, please wash your hands, eh? — remove as many bones and carrots and celery as you can find in there and put them into your triple plastic bag. Then strain the rest into your big pots. Toss the solid bits.

Wash your stock pot and return the stock to it. You may separate this stock into separate containers for freezing now if you want to make different soups down the road, but the proportions for my recipe are for the whole batch.

Bring the stock back up to a boil for 10 minutes.

Meantime, rinse off your beans or rice or pasta or lentils or whatever (any or all) of these you are wanting to add. Rinse them well. The beans (not lentils) will take about an hour or so. You can check them by fishing one out and squishing it. If it squishes, the beans are done. Put beans in first, the rice next, then the pasta or lentils if you're using them, kind of spaced out cooking-time-wise.

Add the beans near the end of this 10-minute boiling period. They will slow things down for a bit but we want to bring them to a boil for about 10 minutes, too. Then turn the heat back to get that gentle simmer with a few bubbles.

Slice your carrots and celery and put those in.

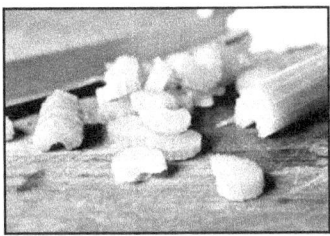

Your other onion can be peeled, sliced in half then sliced into half-rings and put in. I prefer to have large-ish pieces as it looks more "hearty" that way. If you like onions, use two. Or three. Your little half potatoes can go in now, too.

Add your flavourings: parsley (tsp.), sage (1/2 tsp.), thyme (1/2 tsp.), savory (tsp.), basil (1/2-3/4 tsp.), salt if you use it.

After an hour or so, add the 3 bags of frozen vegetables. Wait until the temperature comes back up to that magic temperature then add your 3 cans of Crushed Tomatoes.

This is when you will need to stir it as the tomatoes sometimes stick to the bottom and can burn so best to turn down the temperature a bit and keep a good eye on things.

When everything is cooked through, then you can add:

Cayenne pepper (1/8 tsp.)

Tabasco sauce (shake, shake, shake, shake, shake STOP)

Let it simmer for another 10 minutes or so, turn the burner off, wait for it to cool and then fill your containers with the soup (there will be lots of stuff near the bottom so you'll need a long-handled ladle to get these containers to have a nice balance of ingredients).

Enjoy!

December 21, 2012

Already Dark . . .

And I haven't wished you guys a Happy Solstice.

Been working with the consequences of upgrading to Windows 8 (on both my PC and my laptop!) since maybe 7 AM? gaaa I love AVG but it got twitchy with the download of Windows 8 so had to re-purchase the em-effer and they didn't even acknowledge that I had already bought the whole 2013 year's worth of AVG. [*sigh*] Not yet, anyway. Beats Windows because everybody on the planet who's a hacking asshole tries to get past Windows. My IT guy told me that you can have as many anti-virus programs as you want on your system, but only one Firewall. Well, it appears that AVG now adores the Windows Firewall. Or is that a lie?

Oh, well, everything is working well now and my security system has the equivalent of the A-Bomb in the wings.

Did yaz all like the soup?

Solstice. The day lengths are changing from here on in. Woohoo. Yay!

However . . . If you have downloaded the Calendars I suggested way back when (http://www.sunrisesunset.com/predefined.asp), you will notice that the sun is starting to set later than usual by a minute or so every couple of days — but that the sunrise is later and later by just as many minutes. Poo! But then, miraculously, on January 5, the sunrises start to start earlier. OMG!

You know? Those ancient peeps were really, really on to when the sun rose and set, eh? Like the Maya with their calendar that just happened to end yesterday. The Egyptians laid out their pyramids according to the sun, as well. Maybe there were a lot of people back then who had seasonal depression . . .

Here's a picture of my earrings made by a Maya:

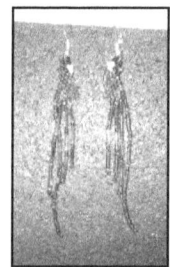

It's the national bird of Guatemala, the Quetzal. I think they're adorable! And since we are still "feeling like we are still here" I can wear them when I want.

This apocalypse thing about the Maya calendar is an excellent lead into my topic of Outer Darkness that I promised on my website . . . Will get to it when I can. Dog-sitting tomorrow for a bit. Then home, then a marathon of SINGING on Christmas Eve and Christmas morn with the choir.

December 26, 2012

Outer Darkness

You see depictions of Outer Darkness as flaming hell and horrible images. Just do a SEARCH and you'll see all kinds of weird things. These are not true, of course. It's all propaganda geared toward scaring the poo out of you so you'll keep going to the church of your choice.

Here you will find a link to a Synopsis of The Soul Eaters http://crowecreations.ca/christina/screenplays.html which is more or less what Outer Darkness is like. Yeah. I wrote a screenplay about it, as in what would happen (although unlikely) if the "levels" got kinda jumbled together for some reason . . . heh heh (I have to figure out how to get the whole screenplay up on my blog here in PDF format . . . Patience, Grasshopper. Which means, I have to remember how I got the link up on my website in the first place. This was a couple of years ago and my memory fades. Poo!)

Main thing is, though, that Outer Darkness is no different from here. Not really. It is, but it's not.

Back in the "old days" (that sounds funny), the Jehovah's Witnesses were predicting that the world was going to end in 1975. Familiar? Compare with Maya?

Thing is, though, it did and nobody noticed. And I think it did on Dec 21, 2012, too. I was just sitting there and suddenly I noticed that everything seemed a little . . . what? brighter? Yes. Brighter. And I felt happy.

If you watch those Quantum Physics shows on Discovery Channel and some of the other channels, you'll see where these guys talk about not so much the possibility but the probability of extra dimensions. That maybe it wasn't so much a Big Bang but that we kinda oozed in from a next-door-neighbouring dimension type thing. I think this concept is cooler than chocolate ice cream!

January 1, 2013

Drool Away! Healthy Soup!

Over the last week, I cooked oodles of stuff (took photos).

I cooked a chicken just so I could use its body (bones) for my soup. bwahahaha

Before:

After:

All the bones and flavourings
doing their thing in my stock pot:

Beans soaking:

(Actually, the beans I made into their own Beans Thing and
ended up with 7.5 litres of them. Didn't use beans in the soup.)
(Oh, and I picked that orange floater off before using these.)

A container of the finished product. Yummy looking, eh?

The amount of soup I ended up with.

I also made a whole whack of rice (no photos of that as everybody knows what long grain white rice looks like) and froze that too. Oh, some of it I put in the 2 meatloaves I made yesterday, sliced thickly, and froze separately, too.

May 2013 bring all kinds of happy surprises to all of you.

January 7, 2013

Dealing with Difficult People

Those of us who deal with depression often have a skewed view of the term "difficult people". When I'm in My Bad Time, I know bloody well that I'm the one who's causing the problem(s). Must be me. After all, I'm the stupid one, the ugly one, the one with no redeeming qualities whatsoever. Right? Baaaaaaa!

I hate to burst your bubble but there actually are assholes out there. Quite a few, in fact. (See below.)

So. Difficult people. Let's say, at work you deal pretty much with

10 fellow employees. One of them is always making somebody feel uncomfortable or unhappy, maybe even especially you. He or she probably is the "difficult" one, then.

But let's say that if of these 10 fellow employees 9 of them make you feel uncomfortable or unhappy, then you're the one with the problem. Get help. This doesn't mean you are bad or fucked up beyond repair or anything. The thing is, if you DON'T go out there and get help, you might end up doing something dumb.

Exception

There are always exceptions, aren't there? If you are a politician and the other 9 difficult people are politicians, too, then maybe it isn't you after all. Same if you are dealing with folks in Big Business. And then, of course, there's the workplace bully. (Odds are against all 9 of them being "difficult", but it's possible.) And there's also the school bully which appears, more and more, recently, to be making young people kill themselves just to get away from them. Not good. Not good at all!

I did some research on psychopaths/sociopaths a couple of years ago for a movie I was writing — The Bus to Siento (which is for sale or option). According to what I found, 1 in 25 people is a psychopath/sociopath. (A psychopath is born that way; a sociopath is made that way. Nature vs. nurture. And no, it's not genetic. and no, they don't all end up as serial killers.) According to one of several articles I read, these numbers are increasing. Interesting. I might do some more research on this phenomenon and let you know.

Psychopaths/sociopaths want one or more of: money, sex, power, control. They have no conscience; they feel no guilt; they do not look ahead at consequences, they only want immediate revenge. Etc., etc.

Here's a link: http://www.exitsupportnetwork.com/artcls/socio.htm

On my website (http://crowecreations.ca/christina/shit_happens.html), I say:

A biggee: If you end up feeling bad about yourself after hanging out with certain people, don't hang out with them anymore. I give you permission to walk away from them. Better lonely than dead.

But sometimes you can't just walk away. Especially if it involves your job, your income. First of all, check out what I suggested to see if it could possibly be "just you" — and then deal with that — but if it isn't just you, then . . . Well. When I was searching for a graphic to go with this post, I ran into dozens and dozens of pieces on how to deal with difficult people. I am not about to cite them all.

Hey! Do your own research. If you constantly rely on others to do stuff for you, your self-esteem will plummet. Doing your own research is actually a lot of fun and you end up knowing a lot of shit that nobody else knows. Nya nya.

However!

If you are living with someone who fits the following description, screw the job, screw the income and get the hell out!

I can't find the link for this bit so will just include it here and apologize for the extra-long post.

I did NOT write this. I found it on the Internet as part of a longer article:

THE MALIGNANT PERSONALITY:

These people are mentally ill and extremely dangerous! The following precautions will help to protect you from the destructive acts of which they are capable.

First, to recognize them, keep the following guidelines in mind.

1) They are habitual liars. They seem incapable of either knowing or telling the truth about anything.
2) They are egotistical to the point of narcissism. They really believe they are set apart from the rest of humanity by some special grace.
3) They scapegoat; they are incapable of either having the insight or willingness to accept responsibility for anything they do. Whatever the problem, it is always someone else's fault.
4) They are remorselessly vindictive when thwarted or exposed.
5) Genuine religious, moral, or other values play no part in their lives. They have no empathy for others and are capable of violence. Under older psychological terminology, they fall into the category of psychopath or sociopath, but unlike the typical psychopath, their behavior is masked by a superficial social facade.

If you have come into conflict with such a person or persons, do the following immediately!

1) Notify your friends and relatives of what has happened. Do not be vague. Name names, and specify dates and circumstances. Identify witnesses if possible and provide supporting documentation if any is available.

2) Inform the police. The police will do nothing with this information except to keep it on file, since they are powerless to act until a crime has been committed. Unfortunately, that often is usually too late for the victim. Nevertheless, place the information in their hands.

Obviously, if you are assaulted or threatened before witnesses, you can get a restraining order, but those are palliative at best.

3) Local law enforcement agencies are usually under pressure if wealthy or politically powerful individuals are involved, so include state and federal agencies as well and tell the locals that you have. In my own experience, one agency that can help in a pinch is the Criminal Investigation Division of the Internal Revenue Service or (in Canada) Victims Services at your local police unit. It is not easy to think of the IRS as a potential friend, but a Swedish study showed that malignant types (the Swedes called them bullies) usually commit some felony or other by the age of twenty. If the family is wealthy, the fact may never come to light, but many felonies involve tax evasion, and in such cases, the IRS is interested indeed. If large amounts of money are involved, the IRS may solve all your problems for you. For obvious reasons the Drug Enforcement Agency may also be an appropriate agency to approach. The FBI is an important agency to contact, because although the FBI does not have jurisdiction over murder or assault, if informed, they do have an active interest in any other law enforcement agencies that do not follow through with an honest investigation and prosecution should a murder occur. Civil rights are involved at that point. No local crooked lawyer, judge, or corrupt police official wants to be within a country mile if that comes to light! It is in such cases that wealthy psychopaths discover just how firm

the "friends" they count on to cover up for them really are! Even some of the drug cartel biggies will scuttle for cover if someone picks up the brick their thugs hide under. Exposure is bad for business.

4) Make sure that several of your friends have the information in the event something happens to you. That way, an appropriate investigation will follow if you are harmed. Don't tell other people who has the information, because then something bad could happen to them as well. Instruct friends to take such an incident to the newspapers and other media.

If you are dealing with someone who has considerable money, you must realize that they probably won't try to harm you themselves, they will contract with someone to make the hit. The malignant type is a coward and will not expose himself or herself to personal danger if he or she can avoid it.

Good luck!

January 16, 2013

Some Tips for Dealing with Insomnia

This link refers to lowering blood pressure, but there are "side effects" — beneficial ones.

http://www.realage.com/insomnia-and-sleep-problems/sleep-better-naturally?src=edit&chan=high-blood-pressure&con=tip

The extra benefits include lessening of depression. Exactly what we need!

January 20, 2013

Have you noticed?

It's 10 to 5 PM right now (here in Ottawa) and it's still light outside! Yay!

The days are starting incrementally — minute by minute — earlier every day, too. Ohhhh blessed be!

And no, that is not a Cow Jumping Over the Moon. It's a Bull jumping over whatever with the SUN in the background.. Equal rights for fairy tale/rhyme peeps and critters, eh? :-)

February 10, 2013

I have been so bad

I need to be punished. I haven't blogged for . . . How long now?

I have been here sitting around, writing stuff, getting two movie scripts off to possible agents, dog-sitting, singing in the choir, getting reports about my totally dementia-laden mother which (surprisingly) depresses the living doodies out of me, editing books for peeps, getting shit from a postal worker, getting shit from a guy I did a HUMUNGOUS favor for and who didn't recognize the favor but instead accused me of trying to rip him off, getting phone calls and emails from men I thought had 86-ed me ages ago — not easy to cope with when you've 86-ed them back and now like zombies they are here. Not wanting so much to eat my brains but to do the nasty with me . . . Jeesh. Didn't think they "cared". Well! lol Of course they don't "care", but really funny that they actually came back to me wanting to do the dirty when there are . . . [figure, figure, figure] over 3 billion other females on Planet Earth? Makes me wonder, makes me think. Distracts me from writing my blog . . .

So ... I didn't have time to write last week.

So like BEAT me, OK?

(I'm actually OK but have been through a rough effing week. And got stronger because I learned from the stress.)

[*whine*]

Dayum. Beat for the whining! Lol

February 14, 2013

Narrowing It Down

I experimented and came up with something good-to-know!

Was having a Bad Day yesterday feeling not so much guilty but just in plain old self-loathing mode and thinking everybody hates me because they thought I did something wrong. I didn't feel that I had done something wrong, but because they felt I had done something wrong, that set me off.

Doesn't take much some days.

What I did though, was realize that this feeling was more or less all in my head. Not that I could do much about it because it had nothing to do with decisions or choice — how can you change the chemistry of anything merely by wishing? — but perhaps there was a chance I could alter whatever was misfiring in my head like I managed to do last November to get me through The Bad Time.

I went through the list of all the things I did last November. Tried my exercise thing but that only made me feel guilty about not doing it more often. Didn't alter a thing physically/mentally. Then remembered that I had set aside a bottle of L-Theanine, just in case I got a chance to experiment with it.

Lo and behold! It worked within, I'd say 20 minutes. I was back up to my happy, fuck-you-if-you-think-that-way-about-me-that's-your-problem-not-mine mode and I even had a very happy sleep last night and nice dreams about handsome young strangers falling in love with me. How nice is that for a change?

So. L-Theanine works for me.

February 24, 2013

It Feels So Good When it Stops?

I am very used to having The Black Cloud of Guilt follow me around starting June 21-ish and increasing in intensity until December 1 then dissipating almost instantly. But something has happened that has really thrown me for a loop.

As I wrote last week, I was having some minor problems with The Usual Crap so decided to get back to taking L-Theanine (125 mg x 2 per day of the straight stuff, not the "with Green Tea" type).

Surprise, surprise! I woke up not once, but three then four then five days in a row and STILL without The Black Cloud of Guilt even the slightest little itsy bit — not a whiff of it even — hanging over me. But hey, did I rejoice in having this em-effing thing completely gone out of my life since I was maybe 13 years old? Noooo, of course not. I missed it so much I attempted to make myself feel guilty for not feeling guilty. "Surely to gawd there's something I've done wrong. Well yeah, there's that [a silly minor thing], but I can't make myself feel guilty about that. Oh dear. What am I going to do with myself if I don't wake up fighting guilt every morning? What will be my new routine?"

That damned Black Cloud of Guilt isn't there at all.

What has replaced it is a feeling that I'm missing something that I've had with me for many, many years. The warning lights are going off telling me to be cautious not to create a scenario that will resurrect it. I've run into people who have grown up in extremely dysfunctional homes with lots of fighting and arguing and hurting and pain. These people often grow up needing a constant supply of excitement in their lives. I think you know the type. People who've never been there call them Drama Queens/Kings. That's not fair because they can't help it — well, they can — because it removes so much from their lives, they feel empty.

Maybe we need to take advice from amputees and learn from them how to deal with what we are now missing. I am not diminishing what amputees must deal with. Please don't get me wrong. But missing a part of what we think is "us" is mentally equivalent.

March 21, 2013

This is where I was

It is always beautiful out in the boonies with nothing but rocks and trees around. We had a big snowfall in the area last week so when I went out with the dogs, after the wild turkeys had left, there was a clean pallet for footprints.

I spotted tracks made by a single deer walking by just past those bushes on the other side of the turkeys. And there were rabbit prints, too. The rabbit was taking his time as well.

I am regenerated!

I often wonder what the budgies make of their giant cousins . . .

April 7, 2013

April 7 already!

Easter Week was a marathon. We sang from Wednesday to Sunday. I am fully recovered, however. Even from the special service on Saturday night — the Vigil — which is beautiful but.

But? Why a but? At the beginning of the service (10 PM), all the lights in the church, including the choir loft, are shut off and then, from the back of the church, one by one, each white taper is lit until the whole church is alight with candles. It would give anybody a rush, I'm sure, to see it.

After several prayers, the lights come back on, the choir sings Gloria loud enough to make the roof lift a bit, and the people sit and extinguish their candles and the regular Mass ensues . . .

. . . while the smoke from the extinguished candles drifts upwards to hang there in the rafters of the huge church — and in the choir loft.

This is usually not bad as the smoke is not too awfully thick. However, this year, the new priest thoughtfully kept re-lighting everybody's candles every time a new section of the Mass came up and the people stood to pray. Then out with the candles and up with more smoke.

A burning candle gives off little smoke, but putting it out makes all kinds of smoke rise. One candle isn't too bad, but a couple of hundred of them — times THREE I might add! — can send quite a bit of smoke up into the higher reaches of a church. Like the choir loft!

Most of the other guys did OK but I have emphysema. Not major emphysema. Not yet! But every time I breathe in smoke, more little thingeys in my lungs get fried. By Mass end, I had to sit down just to maintain an airway. Wow. Scary! I was still not at full capacity the next morning for Mass but after several allelujahs and that wonderful loud Gloria again, I was able to expel quite enough residual candle smoke and get back up to par by mid-Mass.

Bottom line? If you don't smoke, don't start and if you do smoke, stop before it's too late.

April 27, 2013

I Am SO Going on Vacation!

I have a couple of days coming up where I will be in the semi-country with a buncha doggies — four of whom are newly arrived on Planet Earth, i.e., one of them turned a day old around noon today.

Am I gonna love it?

You betcha!

I will report later.

May 12, 2013

Busy, busy, busy

Got my dog-sitting gig done and came back home to . . . yes, a list like this To Do. So I have a good excuse for not posting. (Except that my blog is on that list. Bad me.)

The most wonderful news is that I finally got that latest script finished! Yay. Working title is Skin Eater and the logline is: "A teenage troublemaker learns what racism really is when he stumbles upon the lair of a serial killer."

That's my 3rd script honed since I resigned from doing that e-mag I was telling you about last fall. Apparently, I need to write 7 more before I get any good. [*sigh*] This creates a dilemma because I have a pile of scripts-to-write so am now wondering which one I should leave until last so it will be the best.

I am still alive. But the buggers changed my "person" that comes to see me every week — the last one was with me for about three years! — so I was a bit stressed out worrying if the new person might be the type who figures depression can be cured by either exorcism or herbal soup (although diet does play a role). Seems I lucked out again in getting another really nice person. And an animal lover, to boot!

June 21st fast approaches so wish me luck that I can get through another year from then until December 1 with my new person and all I learned from last year's success. (I am still taking L-Theanine and the hormone replacements.)

On a non me me me note, I was at an 80th birthday party today for a woman who is a Holocaust survivor and a recent recipient of the Governor General's Award. What a privilege it is to be counted among this woman's circle of friends. Wow. She is an amazing woman.

June 8, 2013

Been having a not good time lately

Lots of weather means lots of non-light.

I hope and pray that the peeps in the path of Andrea will be OK!

And I also hope and pray that any of us Depressives in the "path" (non-light) of Andrea will also be OK.

I've had my light on. It's helping.

But I'm also dealing with some shit — but have actually found a "best friend"! Wow! And she's in the choir too and knows the guy I'm going to write about.

Story: One of the guys in the choir has been flirting with me — like for 3 years now. Bless his heart.

He finally got the nerve to ask me if I wanted a drive home after

184 | Christina Crowe

practice about 6 weeks ago. I thought I might as well give him a chance even though I know that pretty much any man born prior to 1947 has this "View" of women that I WILL NOT ACCEPT. But hey. Not fair to judge them all. Right?

So, three weeks ago he expects a kiss. I asked him "Should we really cross that line?" I am thinking that since we "work" together we should not. He says. "Yes!" All horny and everything and this guy is 78 years old.

So I say, "I don't know you. I don't kiss men I don't know."

Grab, grab but no actual lips or anything, just light in the eye.

Oh, by the way, my mother always told me "When you think you see love light in a man's eye, that's not love light, that's tail light.

OK? So I got that.

I say to him. "Listen. You don't know me." (Meaning he has no fucking clue what he's dealing with. That I am a woman who will NOT cook and clean for some guy just because most other women will. That also, I have been sexually assaulted, physically assaulted, have had a loaded gun pointed at me — and an unloaded gun pointed at me — and went through 17 years of some asshole (one of the rapists) treating me like I'm "for him". And that I have a fairly high IQ and like sex a lot but like to play and not just have some jerk ejaculate inside me after two or three kisses which are actually to get HIM aroused enough to get off . . .

The guy says to me "That doesn't matter if you just want to have fun."

Aw shit. You just blew it. I did not say to him "You mean if the MAN just wants to have fun?"

Anyway, I think he got the hint when I said "If you push me, I will run very fast away."

It seemed to me that he had accepted that he would have to wait because he sort of turned away.

Just as I turned to grab the handle to get out of the car, he grabbed my breast.

I've had more things than my breasts grabbed. Trust me on that. But the thing that HURT the most was that he took what he wanted anyway.

I'm still recovering three weeks later. Goodbye, nasty man. I thought you liked me.

July 10, 2013

Here I am. I'm not dead or anything

But I must say that bit about the breast-grabbing took a round out of me.

Then we've had all kinds of overcast days, smog to KILL ya, and the heat! Waaa The heat has been bad so I've had to close the drapes (sunlight) to survive that . . . And June 21 has passed so the days are getting shorter.

Doo!

Not easy so have been having some "symptoms". Poo.

And it also appears that this Blog has been high-jacked by assholes wanting to advertise whiter teeth and shit like that which OVERRIDES what I'm writing. Piss me off or what! It's a bleeding wonder we depressives don't kill more people, eh? Miracles abound.

July 24, 2013

I've been just a little ray of sunshine lately, eh?

But now that there are more rays of actual sunshine — and less heat, and the tech was in yesterday morning to clear up my Malware problem (so now I can Blog again) — things are much better mood-wise for me. I was even able to get out and about yesterday and run a couple of errands. Amazing what a little sidewalk dust will do for a person. And to realize that outdoors still exists! I have errands to run today, too. And I have several projects on the go. Couple of dog gigs coming up next month, too, so looking forward to a big shot of serotonin there, too.

One of my projects is getting a video/commercial/pitch made (need help with that for sure) for the Oaxaca Film Fest (http://www.oaxacafilmfest.com/) that will run from September 21–28 this year and that is because I placed in the top 10% with my screenplay, *The Bus to Siento*. What a thrill to get that news! Wow. The last 7 years of hard work and study and writing have not been in vain. (btw, it's written under my real name name so you won't spot "Christina Crowe" in that list.)

July 25, 2013

The magic bullet against depression?

Spotted some amazing news on Facebook yesterday. Look at this! The magic bullet is in the future: "Scientists discover the molecule responsible for causing feelings of depression." Seems that stress has a lot to do with our bodies producing these nasty hormones/chemicals.

http://www.independent.co.uk/news/science/scientists-discover-the-molecule-responsible-for-causing-feelings-of-depression-8724471.html

Wouldn't it be loverly?

Not sure how it would work for us folks who just need more serotonin, but not having to battle the other junk spewing out constantly would be a huge relief.

August 12, 2013

10 Things You're Wrong about — Yes. That, too.

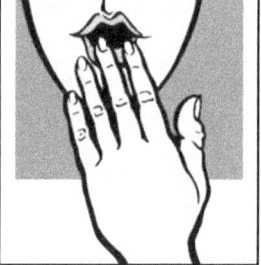

Wow. Check this out! It's right on!

http://www.huffingtonpost.ca/anne-theriault-/living-with-depression_b_3726949.html?icid=maing-grid7|canada|dl1|sec1_lnk1%26pLid%3D356561

I'm still guilty of a few of these.

August 16, 2013

Just a Reminder of Things that Might Help You, too

I posted the list below last October and I am pretty much doing all this already. Had a few bad days this summer when the weather had the clouds blocking out the sunlight. It took a week or so to recover from those days even with getting up at 6:00-ish and turning on my light so I'm being extra cautious because I don't like feeling it so early in the year (June, July).

I am noticing also, that I am closing the draperies earlier and earlier every day. Does it work that fast after December 21 going the opposite direction? Amazing how a minute less of sunlight in a day can push people like us to the edge of The Pit, or a minute more can provide a certain amount of hope and relief.

As mentioned in that previous post, I planned to try eliminating the L-Theanine and I did — twice — and both times I noticed a measurable difference Guilt-Cloud-wise. In the bastid floated! So YES! L-Theanine does have a beneficial effect for me. Suggest you try it. My family physician had a look into it and he didn't jump up and down screaming "Poison" or anything like that, so if it's an OK substance as far as he's concerned, I am more than comfortable recommending it to others.

He recommended I up my Vitamin D to 2000 IUs a day; and I have continued with the 250 mcgs of B12

Just add exercise to this list and you're good to go for another season. Good luck!

I'm up at 5:30 or 6:00 AM to turn on my day (http://www.nor thernlighttechnologies.ca/#!__products/sadelite).

If it's sunny, I turn it off around 11:00 AM; if cloudy, I leave it on.

This is the different thing: I turn it on about a half hour before sunset (calendar here: http://www.sunrisesunset.com/) and leave it on until 8:30 even though it is shining right into my eyes when I'm trying to watch TV. I actually can't wait until 8:30 comes! But I am diligent about it.

I'm taking hormone replacements (estradiol). Research tells me it can boost mood. The literature tells me there are all kinds of precautions go along with this stuff. Hormone replacement can work for males, too (testosterone, in their case, of course), but men have to be very careful about dosages, etc., too, as it can cause a number of things including heart attacks and cancer. Neither of these should be a belly-up-to-the-pharmacy-counter pig-out. Doctor prescription and doctor monitoring only for any of these medications.

I've decided to continue with the L-Theanine (125 mg x 2/morning) [or one tablet of 225 mg/d; check the dosage on the bottle]. I'll maybe remove it when I'm deep into The Bad Time (mid-November) to see if my Guilt Cloud suddenly floats in to besiege me. If it does (float in), then I'll know that the L-Theanine is helping keep it at bay. But maybe I'll wait until next year — or some week in the summer that has several dark days in a row. These affect me, too.

I've bumped up my B12 a notch, too. I'll be taking 250 until December 1. December 1 is when the Guilt Cloud goes away. It will be interesting to see this year, if all my aches and pains disappear at that time, too. I never paid much attention to that. The Guilt Cloud is what I want to escape from as it appears to be what produces that feeling of . . . being nothing of value.

Many people think that depression has to do with sadness. We Depressives know that's not true. But a really hearty laugh can produce oodles of serotonin so the opposite of sad can help us a lot.

August 29, 2013

Sleep cycles and Melatonin

Melatonin changes can cause seasonal depression.

http://www.webmd.com/sleep-disorders/tc/melatonin-overview

I will experiment and let you know it goes.

August 30, 2013

Melatonin and depression

On second thought, I ain't gonna TOUCH the stuff!

http://scholar.google.com/scholar?q=melatonin+and+depressio
n&hl=en&as_sdt=0&as_vis=1&oi=scholart&sa=X&ei=dpcgU
v_lLJLH4APz0oCYCw&sqi=2&ved=0CCcQgQMwAA

I know it's hard reading — scientific papers have their own
"language" — but do your best to wade through this stuff. And be
veeerrrrry careful about taking Melatonin supplements if you
have depression issues. Unless, of course, your doctor
recommends it in your case.

Apparently that link doesn't work for some folks. Here are some more in case:

http://psycnet.apa.org/psycinfo/1988-32953-001

http://www.gwern.net/Melatonin

http://www.sciencedirect.com/science/article/pii/003193849190336M

http://www.ncbi.nlm.nih.gov/pubmed/10420439

http://www.ncbi.nlm.nih.gov/pubmed?term=melatonin%20and%20depression&itool=QuerySuggestion

To read most of the scientific articles, one needs to individually subscribe. I am not able to do that from here. The Abstract and Conclusion will be beneficial though.

September 5, 2013

Because of this . . .

http://www.thedoctorwillseeyounow.com/content/depression/ar
t3473.html?getPage=2#topic2

I got myself one of these (check out the Lumie):

http://www.northernlighttechnologies.ca/#!__products/lumie

Do some research on Melatonin! Wow. Didn't think that crud had
so much CONTROL over my brain. Jeepers!

I received my Lumie yesterday. Played with it/set it up and it did its thing last night and this morning. And I cannot believe it! I woke up with NO GUILT CLOUD this morning (which has been nibbling at me lately, the bastid). And was in a pretty happy mood all day and still am. Hmm.

Suggest you give it a shot.

Smoking doodies! Maybe it's all about the melatonin . . .

September 7, 2013

It's Working!

Three days now I've used my new Lumie BodyClock and have awakened in a happy, liking-myself mood. No Guilt Cloud whatsoever. Amazing.

Here's a video about it:

http://www.youtube.com/watch?v=pO5Tcr3OpC8 (This is the one I have.)

Here are some different models:

http://www.lumie.com/collections/all

Mine's the one on the right. I'm so pleased with the results already, that I even want to hug the picture!

I have learned how to make the wake-up sounds work now. What wakes me up — besides the cat walking on my hair — is now the twittering of birds. It's a repeated sound so gets annoying enough that it will wake you up to turn it off so no danger of sleeping through it. (There's also a rooster sound; waves; white noise; and a regular beep beep.

I have set the alarm for 6:00 AM and the light to start sixty minutes before that. It gradually lights up the room and by 6:00 it is fully bright and the bird songs chime in.

At night, I let it wind down for maybe 20 minutes as I go to sleep. It's odd, but just as the data on melatonin says (melatonin helps the sleep cycle), I can feel myself getting sleepier as the light gets dimmer. As I dozed off last night, my last thought was: "Gonna have to tell my Blog Guys about thisszzzzz . . ."

September 18, 2013

So far so good . . .

Eleven more days of success with the Lumie 250!

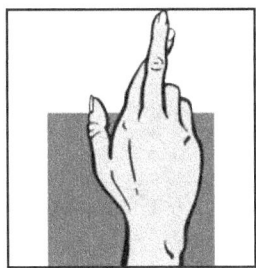

Not even a wisp of The Guilt Cloud and it's well into September. It usually starts following me around in August — sometimes July as it did this year. This year has been especially bad because it's been so overcast.

For those of you who missed the link in a previous post, this is the Northern Light Technologies Home page:

http://www.northernlighttechnologies.ca/#!__home

And this is one is for the Lumie 250 itself:

http://www.northernlighttechnologies.ca/#!__products/lumie

I am now using the Lumie 250 in conjunction with my SADelite. I don't know what I'd do without my SADelite. I use it as ambient light and have set it up near-ish the window where I work.

If you don't work from home, then you use it for about half an hour in the mornings as illustrated in this page:

http://www.northernlighttechnologies.ca/#!__products/sadelite

I would suggest, when you get home after work, you turn it on until perhaps 8:00 or 9:00 PM. Check out on your sunrise/sunset calendar (http://www.sunrisesunset.com/) what time the sun goes down in your area during the last month you felt good. This, of course, is principally for fellow SAD sufferers but since sunlight helps the body produce serotonin, it can't hurt for regular depression. Every little bit helps.

I've used the SADelite for years but until last year, I was turning it off when I closed the draperies when it got dark outside (it was on the window sill). Last year, I tucked the draperies around behind it and started the strict 6:00 AM to 8:30 PM regimen and had no thoughts of suicide last year whatsoever. Allelujah! First November since I can remember — and I am talking about back in my teens.

Good luck with this and I hope it helps you, too. Let us know.

September 29, 2013

Well that was fun. Not.

A week or so ago on The Young and the Restless, retired military guy, "Dylan", had a PTSD (Post Traumatic Stress Disorder) episode involving an infant. The loss of what he had believed to be his son — making this the second of his children that he lost (one was miscarried) — triggered the wartime memory of not being able to save a young girl from death.

"Dylan" didn't know where he was. He didn't know that the baby in his arms was a very young baby boy and not the little girl he had been unable to save.

http://en.wikipedia.org/wiki/Posttraumatic_stress_disorder

My recent PTSD flashback episodes (the breast grab — dealt with and overcome — and something that happened on Wednesday) were nothing like this, but they were nonetheless real. Let me be clear that the "flashback" was to the emotional state, not some hallucination where I was back there again. Although my dreams these last few days have not been pleasant ones, so maybe.

I've been doing very well with my new Lumie bodyclock (http://www.northernlighttechnologies.ca/#!__products/lumie) and no, I don't have shares in this company, so it was a surprise to wake up feeling antsy on Thursday morning and even until this morning (Sunday).

But no Guilt Cloud. Can I get a resounding and most happy "YAY!" from all y'all?

I am very happy to announce that having this latest PTSD episode helped me understand something. Sometimes I'm fighting two demons: one is Depression, the other is recovery from an abusive relationship. Often the twain do meet but they're essentially separate things. However . . .

Yes, however, because one of the symptoms of Depression is risk taking, we often find ourselves in situations that are dangerous for us mentally and/or physically. Many times when I am attempting to explain my Depression to people, they grab onto what I went through during those 17 years of abuse and come up with comments like: "Oh, no wonder. You poor thing, you."

No. I'm not a poor thing. I made that choice all on my own. This could possibly make me a brave thing, yes? (See, I refuse to call myself "stupid" anymore so let's call me brave — although foolhardy suits much better.)

Although I am still feeling uncomfortable since Wednesday, my Depression is still at bay. This is good. We'll see what will happen around October 26 which is usually the time when the Guilt Cloud, the aches and pains, the I-don't-give-a-shit-about-anything sledge hammer swings in.

October 2, 2013

Larks vs Night Owls & a Depression Connection

Interesting . . .

Just collected this from Facebook courtesy of I Fucking Love Science:

http://www.newscientist.com/article/dn24292-first-physical-evidence-of-why-youre-an-owl-or-a-lark.html#.UkwxjVNdyPP

October 14, 2013

Thanksgiving Day in Canada 2013

And I am thankful indeed for having discovered the Lumie 250 Bodyclock. This is a picture of the box.

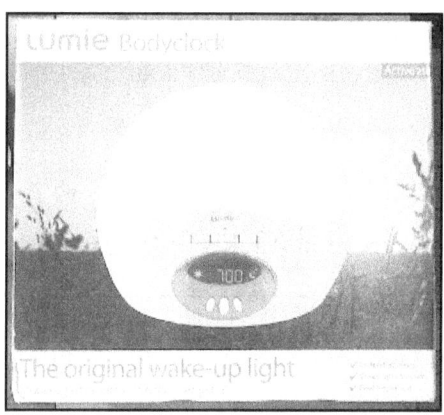

It's a miracle. It truly is. My head is clear. There are no dark thoughts, no "black dogs" jumping around in my head 24/7 starting in July and peaking from October 26-ish to December 1 and making me fight the constant urge to kill myself to make all the guilt and hatred I am feeling from others (non-existent) stop.

I've heard others say "I just wanted it all to go away."

As usual during My Bad Time, I now have The Stupids and my body hurts — so My Bad Time is definitely here (as of October 3 this year) — but there's no Guilt Cloud and I am craving salads (a summertime thing) rather than carbs.

The only drawback is that I sometimes don't know what day it is. And I also assume that it's nice and warm outside. A small price to pay for relief!

I have a Weather App on my computer and when I see that the temperature is 9 or 10°C (48 or 50°F) I look out the window and say, "No it's not. It's really nice out. What's going on? Ah, of course! My body thinks it's July." And this is exactly what I want it to think so it will stop with that extra melatonin production.

I have my Lumie set up so sunrise starts at 5:15 AM and gradually brightens until the chirping bird alarm starts at 6:00 to wake me. (The Lumie alarm can be set for an FM radio station, a rooster, waves, or white noise.) I immediately go into the living room/office and turn on the main SADelite which fills the room with sunshine.

What I find interesting is that when the light gets bright enough to wake me on its own (around 5:40 or so), I grumble and roll over, but when the birds start and I open my eyes at 6:00, I am fully awake and rarin' to go. And happy about it. Full of energy.

At 8:30–9:00 PM, I turn off the SADelite in the living room and in no time I am sleepy and ready for bed.

Some links again are:

http://www.northernlighttechnologies.ca/#!__products/lumie

http://www.thedoctorwillseeyounow.com/content/depression/art3473.html?getPage=2#topic2

http://scholar.google.com/scholar?q=melatonin+and+depression&hl=en&as_sdt=0&as_vis=1&oi=scholart&sa=X&ei=dpcgUv_lLJLH4APz0oCYCw&sqi=2&ved=0CCcQgQMwAA

http://psycnet.apa.org/psycinfo/1988-32953-001

http://www.gwern.net/Melatonin

http://www.sciencedirect.com/science/article/pii/003193849190336M

http://www.ncbi.nlm.nih.gov/pubmed/10420439

http://www.ncbi.nlm.nih.gov/pubmed?term=melatonin%20and%20depression&itool=QuerySuggestion

October 26, 2013

Not a Cure, a Circumvention!

Imagine, if you will, waking up every single day since childhood between October 25 and November 30 with the most horrible feeling that you have done something so terribly bad that you deserve to die and your tiny circle of acquaintances won't even notice you're gone.

Now imagine waking up at 5:30 AM one morning in Ottawa Canada on October 26 with a smile on your face and feeling that you are in love with the whole world and the whole world is in love with you. Nothing extreme, merely peaceful, eager to meet the challenges of the day, and thinking to yourself: Holy shit. It WORKS! My new light works! Allelujah!

Now I just have to figure out how to deal with the other symptoms of depression: The Stupids and the aches and pains.

And boy, oh, boy! do I have aches and pains. I think it's called the levator scapula (it's the muscle running from the back/side of the neck to behind the V of the bones on top of the shoulder, right where your purse strap sits if you carry one). That muscle had me almost vomiting with pain Thursday night and Friday morning. I ended up taking painkillers all day — which I hate to do so that just goes to show you how much it hurt. I have a very high pain threshold so I think it would have brought most people to their knees. (But it did take my mind off my achy hips, so that's a good thing.)

Would I exchange that pain for The Guilt Cloud? Not on your life! Not on my life.

I'm not saying I have pain IN PLACE OF The Guild Cloud that is no longer following me around, what I'm saying is that now that The Guilt Cloud is out of the way, I can feel the rest of me.

The Stupids? It's actually kind of refreshing to have a relatively empty brain for a change instead of having four million things going on in there all the time. I'll look at The Stupids as a brain vacation from now on.

Conclusion

(don't I sound like a scientist, eh?)

Artificially lengthening the day from 6:00 AM to ~8:30–9:00 PM has a very positive effect on at least one person's physiology. So much so that she recommends her regimen to all who must deal with seasonal depression.

Because I don't deal with year-round depression (although I think I do, but not the suicidal type year round), I don't know if it will work for those who are not affected by shortened daylengths. If there is someone out there who would like to try the 15-hour bright light regimen (Lumie 250 Bodyclock to wake up with and the SADelite or equivalent until ~9:00 PM) to see if it has an effect on them, would they please let us know if it has any effect?

By the way, I am in no way going to stop doing the other things I do to ease my depression. It still lurks there, but I have finally learned how to keep the Black Dogs at bay.

October 30, 2013

Happy Dance!

Those of you who've been following this Blog since it started (Sept 4 2011) will have seen what happens around October 26: the Black Dogs circle, The Guilt Cloud floats in, the fight to get through November begins.

This year?

Nobody showed up.

Yay! Yay! Yay!

Except for Sunday (27th) . . . when it seemed I could not get enough to eat. I couldn't stop eating. I even gave myself a sore stomach. Glad it wasn't beer or I'd still be dealing with the hangover! I had made soup (see soup blog entries:

http://christinacrowe.blogspot.ca/2012/12/how-to-make-really-healthy-broth-part-1.html
http://christinacrowe.blogspot.ca/2012/12/how-to-make-really-health-broth-part-2.html
http://christinacrowe.blogspot.ca/2012/12/how-to-make-good-healthy-soup-part-3.html)

and that's what I ate. Two big containers of it! (And it gets diluted 50 : 50.)

Oh, and some homemade lasagna, too.

Oh, and I had some Lowney Bridge Mixture (http://www.canadianfavourites.com/Lowney_Bridge_Mixture_340g_p/hershey039.htm) left and that half bag disappeared in no time. But, hey. C'mon. Some of those pieces are dark chocolate which is good for us . . . And nuts are good for us, too . . . And there are raisins in there . . .

btw, when you make your own meals from scratch (preferably with free-range and/or Kosher or Halal critters; and vegetables need tender care, too, don't forget), you control what goes into it — especially salt and sugars and MSG and other crud, like preservatives, that nobody needs in their system — and it doesn't do as much damage to overeat something.

The munchies tapered off miraculously and I now have a fridge full — well, not so full anymore — of salads, including tabouli (good healthy stuff).

Yesterday I had a big urge for carbs so bought some white squishy bread and a tin of salmon. Salmon is good for depression. Uh. Maybe I should reword that: "Salmon is not good for depression as it helps make depression go away." Lame attempt at joke. Sorry.

Got home. Got a whiff of the white squishy bread, thought, "Ew," and set it aside and reached for salad. This shows that the light regimen is working at a physical level. Carb urges are much, much lower than usual. Interesting . . .

I will carry on through this year's The Bad Time without making any changes to the other things I have been doing, but maybe next year I will attempt to experiment (I always want to pronounce that word with a Victor Frankenstein accent!) by removing one thing at a time. However, to tell you the truth, I have been so busy lately, I haven't being getting much exercise in; so that has been eliminated by chance.

Hang in there.

November 4, 2013

Define "Angst"

A couple of days ago I woke up with a little teeny bit of . . . what?

Angst! That's what it was. The perfect word, angst: "a feeling of deep anxiety or dread, typically an unfocused one about the human condition or the state of the world in general."

But it went away within maybe 10 minutes.

Yay. That flipping light is still working!

I'm not quite stopping folks on the street to tell them about it, but darn near. Maybe when I run out of friends and acquaintances (and long-suffering, bored relatives), I will go get myself a soapbox and announce it to the heavens.

There are so many people who do not understand what Depression really is. Some think it's merely a profound sadness (mere?); a lack of vitamin D; a bid for attention.

It's a PHYSICAL thing. If this new light can make me crave salads in lieu of carbs at this time of year. Hey.

btw, here's my website: http://crowecreations.ca/christina

November 11, 2013

Tired, Cranky, No Energy . . .

. . . and my body aches, The Stupids reign, I have no enthusiasm and I have the munchies but nothing seems to satisfy my taste buds — I don't know what it is I crave, but it's something. Normally I know exactly.

It is a chore to get up and at 'em every morning now that we are this deep into November.

But That's OK. There is NO Guilt Cloud. Nada. Niente. Gone-o's.

What a relief. An unbelievable load off my shoulders that now hurt like hell all the time.

I don't even feel guilty about sounding like a whiny spoiled brat complaining about all my aches and pains.

The Lumie 250 Bodyclock continues to do its wonderful, wonderful work.

December 1, 2013

I Made It!

Another November conquered and this one without a single blip of the Guilt Cloud.

Bless you Lumie ACTIVE 250 Bodyclock for helping me get to December 1 alive again.

Actually, on Wednesday afternoon (Nov 27), I looked out my window. It was sunny. But there was a difference to the "sunny". It was as though the angle of the sun had shifted. There's an image here: Earth going around the sun that will show you what I pictured and what I think caused it. That the Earth just moved incrementally (relatively speaking!) from one spot to another and it made that big difference.

Tomorrow's post will be "Avoiding People Who Are Bad for Us".

December 2, 2013

Avoiding People Who Are Bad for Us

"Yabut, I love him/her!" we profess with the greatest of conviction. (Because we believe it, too.)

Sorry.

It's the risk we love — that serotonin-producing risk — not that guy or gal we subconsciously know is going to end up giving us heaps of grief eventually. The one I was sure I loved the most did drugs, stole stuff, beat me, stalked me, couldn't hold down a job .

. . Best sex I ever had. How sick is that to go to such risk for a bit of serotonin? I loved him to—? Death?

It got so bad with him, trying to escape from him, that I attempted suicide: pills and cut my wrists the long way. That's when I fried a lot of my left brain.

I've been involved with drunks (several), druggies (one), obsessive-compulsives (most), narcissists (most), sociopaths/psychopaths*, terrorists (one), hebephiles (one), misogynists (probably just the one), sex addicts (one who had it really bad), and pathological liars (one).

You'd think I would have learned.

But I did learn. Once was enough with many of these types. (And by the way, those are individual traits. Most of these people had combos. Example: the terrorist was the druggie; the misogynist was a drunk, a psychopath, a pathological liar, and was compelled to break my stuff whenever he could; the hebephile was a sex addict and a psychopath.)

However . . .

The only ones I repeatedly went back to were the Obsessive Compulsive Personality Disorder (compulsive drinkers fit in here) and the narcissist (socio- and psychopaths fit in here). But I learned how to recognize and avoid those with this "quirk" through a three-year stint with a psychiatrist who gave me a complete run down of "symptoms", the main one being to ask myself: "Is he trainable?" A non-gender-specific gauge would be "Insanity: doing the same thing over and over and expecting different results." — Albert Einstein

I was so very pleased and happy to finally eschew this particular very-bad-for-me-type after all those years of ending up with men who were very difficult to live with. Dealing with my choice of man made me difficult to live with as well. Seesaw anyone? I withdrew, wouldn't play the head games these unbalanced men craved to play.

Guilt, guilt, guilt. Of course it was all my fault.

Of course it was!

I picked them in the first place, didn't I?

So, with all this newfound intelligence about how to recognize, thus avoid, the Obsessive-Compulsive Narcissist in my arsenal, away I went into the world of relationships again only to get myself involved with a pathological liar. Maybe he would be better described as a compulsive liar, but either way, he had a big problem with the truth.

Ask him if it's raining out and he would answer: "No, yes." if it was raining; and "Yes, no." if it wasn't.

This guy was either a sociopath or a psychopath*. It's hard to know whether it was nurture or nature in his case, but either way, I ended up with a guy who did dumb things and blamed them on someone else. I was the handiest. His abuses covered the gamut from sexual through verbal, emotional and mental to financial. Name it. The stereotypical mean drunk and always wanting to pick a fight. (http://www.amazon.com/Games-Alcoholics-Claude-Steiner-Ph-D/dp/0345323831)

Actually, I felt quite sorry for this man. What can be more difficult to deal with than being a heterosexual misogynist?

Looking back on my three-year stint with the psychiatrist, I also remember this psychiatrist's caution: "Eighty percent of humanity is fucked up somehow. The other twenty percent is already taken."

"Dammit!"

Be careful out there. Get your serotonin from eating the right foods, exercise. . . Or from the sun, not from a son-of-a-bitch (or from the bitch who birthed him in the case of guys who run into bad women. And yes, there are bad women out there, too.)

*Note: Even shrinks have trouble spotting a sociopath or psychopath and the thin line between these two species makes it difficult to place the right label on them.

December 25, 2013

Merry whatever

I'll try to get something written in the next few days.

Meanwhile, don't off yourself, OK?

I've been busier than shit! Sorry.

Notice buggy eyes on [busy] bee. (LOL re "buggy" — but actually, that's OK because bees aren't "bugs". Anyway. I'll get back to yaz.)

I was away dog-sitting for 9 days; home for 4; dog-sitting for 9 days; then into singing my ass off with three Masses from Christmas Eve to Christmas Day. (Love that, though! Kept me sane in high school.)

Will get back to you and fill y'all in.

December 26, 2013

The Last Post?

Since I managed to talk/write my way through years and years of seasonal depression over the last two and have come up with a regime that works (for me), I think it's time to put this blog to rest and set it up in book form.

It will be available through Amazon.com in e-book format and in print. The print version will be somewhat pricey if it's in colour. I'd like to maintain the colour because it's bright and shiny. The e-book version will be "in Kindle" but you won't need a Kindle to download it to your computer.

I'll let you know when my designer, Crowe Creations, has set it up, ergo, when it will be available to the public. Eventually, it will be available worldwide through Amazon. Just keep checking for *My Search for Serotonin: Experiences of Suicidal Depression and how to deal with it* by Christina Crowe.

There will be Free Promotion Days for the Kindle version.

Meanwhile, I'll leave you with a little bit of repeated advice.

Symptoms of depression are:

1. promiscuity
2. substance abuse
3. risk taking

Whenever you notice yourself doing any of these things, no matter how good (serotonin-producing) it feels, stop, step back, realize it for what it is, then haul out your lights and your L-theanine and your exercise program and your cans of salmon and tuna, this blog, and realize that you aren't alone. Oh, and your chocolate!

Best of the best of luck to all of you and thanks for being there for me. Yes. Knowing that someone on line was listening helped me a lot.

If this blog has been of any benefit to you, please spread the word about it to others who are dealing with depression, too.